Auctions

For Amateurs

Sandra Quinn-Musgrove
with
Edward J. Doherty

BLUE
HOUSE
PRESS

San Antonio, Texas

Library of Congress Catalog Card Number:
93-71299

Blue House Press
P.O. Box 40217, San Antonio, Texas 78229
ISBN 0-9628295-2-8

Printed in the U.S.A.

Dedicated to the hard-pressed American consumer, who deserves every possible break—including the high values and modest prices available at auction.

INTRODUCTION

Why Auctions?

In good times and bad, everybody loves a bargain. That explains why so many garage sales, yard sales, fire sales, clearance sales, flea markets, and used-goods stores attract throngs. I know no one who hesitates to shop this way. When it comes to attending auctions, many of the same shoppers draw the line. Yet auction-buying is unquestionably the best way to get the quality you want at the absolute bottom price. So what's the hold-up?

The answer's easy: fear of the unfamiliar.

Television has convinced people that: auctions are complicated; you have to learn unintelligible language used by auctioneers; you must master arcane methods of offering bids, using finger language, nods, or other peculiar means of communication; all the procedures are alien and, if you don't know them, you can make a fool of yourself; competition is fervid and unpleasant; you are pressured to pay higher prices than you can afford.

Most of this is rubbish.

Buying at auction *is* different. But it certainly is not difficult. Most auctioneers talk in straightfor-

1

spend much more than you intended."

Finally, said Shari, she loved the experience. "I'm definitely going back to this and other auctions." But, she added, "I'd advise other amateurs to avoid getting there as early as I did. We allowed more than an hour to inspect the merchandise in advance, while 15 minutes would have been adequate."

In short, her first experience was interesting, pleasurable and profitable, as it has proved to be for many others. There was an element of luck, too. Her ignorance of auctions didn't lead her into any traps, as sometimes happens. My purpose in this book is to give you enough know-how in advance to eliminate the need for luck. For those early forays onto the auction scene can just as well prove unlucky unless you are prepared to act with some sophistication.

A colleague of mine got me thinking along these lines one day when he said: "My wife and I go to a lot of garage sales, junk stores and flea markets, and we tried an auction once. We didn't have the slightest idea of what was happening, so we've never gone to another one." I went searching in the library to find a book I could recommend to him and to many others who, when they learn I buy practically everything at auction, start to ask fundamental questions.

There was nothing in the stacks to guide a newcomer to auction-shopping. So was born the idea of my writing what amounts to a primer for men and women who could benefit greatly from attending auctions but are hesitating to try. Writing is part of my work as a college professor and department head, and certainly my inveterate auctiongoing has taught me the ropes.

I have tried to tell the auction story in *Auctions for Amateurs* just as I learned it after having been discouraged by my earliest experiences. It begins at the end, really, by setting forth many examples of experiences my husband Fred and I have had while greatly enriching our lives by acquiring treasures at auction. Fred is as passionate an auction buff as I am. The idea is to help you by providing a wealth of examples.

The story moves on from there to explain what to expect at the many different types of auctions and how to conduct yourself, with tips on how to come out a big winner. There are sections on auctioneers and other personnel, on methodology, and on the red lights to watch for in case you find yourself in the hands of a crooked operator.

You may have asked yourself many questions. "Where do I find an auction? How will I know whether they're selling anything I want? How should I figure out how much to bid? How do I go about registering? How can I find out whether the auction people are honest? What do I actually do once I get there?" It is questions like these I have tried to answer in this book.

Help has come from many sources. Veteran auctiongoers have a tendency to become clannish, and we've come to know and value a great variety of them who have volunteered their own experiences, suggestions and advice to assure this book represents more than one woman's opinion. We have consulted respected auctioneers for their views, talked over organization and planning of the book with knowledgeable colleagues and, when ques-

sents a triumph of some sort. It may fill a niche in the home, satisfy a curiosity, still a suppressed desire, provide the raw material for a project, or simply represent extraordinary value.

It is hard for knowledgeable bargain-hunters to lose at auction-shopping. Only the amateur, the unskilled or the unwary come away from auction sales financially skinned or psychologically scarred. Even a sealed box of unknown content, bought for peanuts, may contain a treasured surprise; it may also turn up useless junk. If you take away no more than this from an auction, you will have had a memorable experience.

"Knowledgeable bargain-hunter" is the key phrase here. It can be risky for the amateur to enter an auction sale without understanding the process. It is possible to be fooled by what appears to be a bargain if you don't understand what you are really looking for. Not all auctions are above-board, and it is important to distinguish straightforward dealers from the few crooked ones.

It is the purpose of this book to enable any reader to attend an auction with considerable assurance that he or she stands to profit from it, rather than suffer loss or disappointment. The lessons here come from one who has made all the mistakes, taken her losses, and learned from dedicated auctiongoing how to avoid error and loss and, instead, to embroider her life with riches attained at little cost through intelligent participation in thousands of auction sales.

My husband Fred and I have bought everything at auction from bricks to vehicles. We have acquired valuable antiques, household appliances, furniture, decorative items, business machines, even clothing. What we can't use ourselves we have given away or sold at a tidy profit. We even have a small guest house on our property that has been turned into a warehouse for auction-purchases that we regularly resell to friends, neighbors or strangers.

For us, attending auctions is more than a hobby but less than a business. We both work at full-time jobs, travel and vacation a lot and enjoy an active social life. We regard attending auctions as a challenge, an ever-surprising adventure, and a means of stretching our rather ordinary income to cover what many others would consider luxuries. Yet we do not recommend that readers become such dedicated auction buffs. Some will, of course, who discover a new and satisfying direction to life in the competition and satisfactions of auction bidding. But my main purpose in writing this book is to help many find a new way of enriching their environments by learning how to live better while spending less.

Let me start with an example of just how much value a buyer can wring out of doing his or her buying at auction. This is the true story of how my daughter and I furnished a house from floor to ceiling and living room to kitchen with inexpensive auction bids.

Furnish a House for $1,000?

One of our most challenging tests of the thriftiness of auction-buying was occasioned by the move of our daughter and her husband to our hometown San Antonio, Texas, from their residence in Las Vegas. To finance their move and provide funds until they found work in their new location, they sold their

in. The home is beautifully outfitted, and today, though periodically new pieces are added, or auction purchases are sold to finance another piece, little is changed.

Counting the Gains

It is impossible to calculate precisely how much money we saved by buying at auction. If we had purchased all these items new at retail, the cost would have been something like $5,500. If picked, one by one, at used-furniture stores or flea markets, the price would have been closer to $2,100. In fact, we paid out slightly less than $1,000.

For the benefit of newcomers to the auction adventure, I have compiled a chart, representing our itemized spending, and comparing these prices with the approximate retail and used furniture costs. You will find this in the Appendix.

Furnishing a House Becomes Old Stuff

With this experience behind us, Fred and I were undaunted when we discovered the need to provide housing for an elderly member of the family.

Deciding to give this dwelling a dual function, we purchased a house with two living units; one for our relative and one for ourselves. Moreover, we located the new property in a resort area of the Texas Gulf coast. This served not only the original purpose but it also gave us a fishing getaway for use on frequent weekend jaunts for our favorite pastime. And, since we rent to our relative, we also have another tax write-off to cushion the cost of what will become our retirement home some years from now.

Furnishing these living places became an easy quest because it had little of the urgency of our previous experience.

Again, I have spelled out our costs for the furnishings, along with a comparison with approximate retail prices. This chart too is in the Appendix.

You will find another revealing list in the Appendix. This details quite a number of additional items we have acquired through the years, comparing our cost with the equivalent value of the same items at retail. In it is revealed our most egregious mistake, made very early in our experiences with auctions. In this case our price is compared, not with the retail equivalent, but with the going price at other auctions.

Fred wanted to surprise me with a first wedding anniversary present. On the appointed date a truck arrived and workmen hauled into the house a Thomas solid-state organ, a magnificent instrument, complete with all the stops and two tiers of keys. I loved it and immediately started taking lessons.

Only later did I learn that he had opened wide the checkbook and paid $900 for it. Since then, we've seen identical instruments go at auction for as little as $400. That cert ainly opened our eyes. We vowed never again to make such a major purchase blindly. And it was one of the several experiences that determined us never to attend an auction alone, particularly if we had a major purchase in mind. That's a lesson you too may want to take to heart.

Chapter Two

Nothing Like a Bargain

It's not often in a lifetime that a man or woman has occasion to furnish a house from scratch. But in every life it is common to need or want something that is hard to find, hard to afford, or simply unexpectedly available. And there are hordes of people who are constantly seeking what are to them the raw materials for an entrepreneurial enterprise. Others – call them adventurers of routine existence – simply love to hunt bargains, whether they are needed or not. Auctions satisfy these cravings.

The purpose of attending auctions is of course to beat the money game. I know of no way to do that more surely and with more satisfaction. You can always be a winner if you know what you're doing. And you can take an awful beating if you do not.

As novices, most of us have wound up as both winners and losers. Buying at auction has its own kind of risks, just as it presents unique opportunities to the canny participant. Most of the men and women who are enthusiasts are self-taught; they still bear the bruises of the hard knocks they accumulated while learning how to make auction-buying pay off handsomely.

I can think of no better way to illustrate this than by relating some of my own experiences and those of others. This should help you avoid our stumbles and at the same time perceive the lucrative opportunities open to you.

It doesn't take a lot of money to profit from auction-buying. As you'll see, the expenditure of a few dollars can sometimes reap hundreds for you. Yet the inexperienced can shoot a bankroll unwittingly and wind up with a handful of junk.

In this chapter I will set forth some of our experiences, good and bad. We begin with the good.

The Unicorn Lives

The creative abilities of some individuals amaze me. Often, when talking with fellow auction regulars, ideas that would never occur to me pop up.

Sitting out a part of an auction, an acquaintance and I were chatting. I asked her about the purchase she had made of two rocking horses. Each was rather badly in need of paint and repair. I knew she had no small children or grandchildren. I found that not only had she purchased the two that day, but she regularly sought others at auction. She asked me to look for rocking horses or other children's large play horses. She would pay me for the purchases, plus a bit more, if I found them. (I never saw any, though I continue to look.) "What do you do with them?" I asked. She told me.

She won the bid on the rocking horses that day, paying only $7 for the pair. Her investment was, therefore, only $3.50 each. She explained that she would take them home, strip them of their rockers, paint and the shabby fittings of fake leather stirrups, saddle, and reins. Then her work of converting them to very marketable merchandise could begin.

A can of spray paint, in any color that struck her fancy – she was thinking of doing the day's purchases in white – would be purchased for less than $2 each. (We have often seen spray paint sold at auction, and one time purchased an entire box of 12 for $5.)

Then, using small pieces of fabric collected from auctions, along with jewelry, beads, feathers, sometimes adding other small retail purchases, and using her artistic skills to paint eyes and other marks on her stripped rocking horses, she would convert the horses to "unicorns". She painted styrofoam cones and glued each to a horse's head. She sometimes uses fabric to cover the horn instead of paint. "All of that seems like a lot of work to me," I observed. "I do the work in the evenings, while watching television," she replied.

Once the rocking horses are converted to unicorns, their sale is assured. She sells each to a specialty shop for $125. In turn, the specialty shop charges customers $200 or more, depending on the style and additions my friend makes on a rocking horse. I had no idea that there is a constant call for unicorns. As this is written, unicorns are a decorator fad.

Requests for her completed "designer unicorns" are more than she can, or is willing to, supply. Yet each month, with investments of no more than $30-$40, including the additions she makes paying retail prices, she sells three to four unicorns. The time spent is, she explained, artistically satisfying, and she makes a profit of $250-$400 each month – just by doing something she enjoys.

Though certainly she will never become wealthy from the purchases she makes and converts to unicorns, she is well served with a small amount of extra money each month, and, perhaps most importantly, the opportunity to work at creating something from nothing.

Magic with Fabric

A dealer in second-hand furniture whom I met at an auction had a similar craft. An uninspiring glass-top table with four chairs was put up to bid. The furniture was constructed of metal, shaped to look like artificial cane. The chairs were covered with an off-white plastic fabric. Had we considered making an offer on the merchandise, we would have bid no more than $50. I watched her raise the bid to $80.

Roughly calculating the markup she would have to add to the purchase price, I figured she needed to bring in at least $150 to make her investment worthwhile. However, I did not calculate her creative skills. She explained to me the conversion she would make, using paint and a small store-owned amount of fabric.

Oriental-looking furnishings are big sellers. (fads differ from place to place, and presently "oriental" has a great deal of attraction for furniture buyers and decorators in our area). She will spray-paint the chairs black and re-cover the "snap-out" seats and backs with an oriental fabric. The glass tabletop will be augmented by a set of oriental fabric place mats, with an oriental vase and flowers strategically placed.

She said that with these small additions she will sell it immediately; she has requests for such completed furniture in her regular customer lists. The selling price? $250-$300, and the buyers will consider their purchases bargains. Indeed a fine return on her $80 investment.

This is not for me, and perhaps not for you. But throughout the land, men and women with sharp ideas and the time to shape them into profitable work are finding their raw materials at auctions.

Baubles and Beads

On another occasion, the innocuous contents of the two boxes did not appeal to me at all. Two chest-like containers were listed together. I found that each of the boxes contained hundreds of little drawers. Each of the drawers was filled with jewelry parts: beads, hooks, sequins, earring backs, rolls of waxed strings, and all the other kinds of materials seen on necklaces, bracelets, earrings, and brooches.

There seemed to be a million tiny pieces in the two chests. We talked briefly of what we could do with the goods and, just as rapidly, we discarded any consideration of buying them. Whatever could be done with this stuff would require a kind of work that appeals to neither of us. When the two chests were brought up to bid, apparently most participating in the auction had reached the same conclusion, even the dealers in attendance. Because of the lack of enthusiasm for the chests, there were few bidders. Yet one young women stayed to the end, and won with a bid of $50 for the two chests.

I wonder. Did the young woman begin a business on her investment of $50? She had enough parts for jewelry to supply any small flea-market stall, or enough for many creations that could be sold to specialty stores. Or with the profit she could make from her abilities with such tiny beads and bangles, she could open a store herself. Next a group of stores. One day, will we read of the beginning of some well-known chain that started with a $50 investment in two chests of beads? Improbable? Of course. Possible? Of course! The stuff of dreams. That's another thing that auctions are all about.

One Man's Junk, Another's Jewels

With few exceptions, all items found at auction have a buyer somewhere, if the price is right. Sometimes, even when the price is too high, purchasers still abound. The cliche that one man's junk is another's treasure is certainly true, particularly at general/junk auctions. Some items we have purchased are discards of others. To us, they are treasures. Auction businesses would fail, if this were not a reality. Second-hand stores rely on regular sales of things discarded as ugly, unworkable, broken, or junk.

The value of the junk depends on the buyer's use and sometimes the ability to return the junk to its original quality. If the buyer cannot do the work, he or she must hire others. When this is the case, the costs of restoration should be calculated into the purchase/bid price.

A woman we know well is an auction buff. She makes what she considers "fabulous" buys at auctions. "Really, the price was so low I couldn't turn it down," she explains. She is a successful attorney who has no interest in restoring anything. However, as she often explains about her so-clled fabulous buys, "...but I can afford to have them restored." Her home is a collage of restored "fabulous buys".

We once watched her bid on two kitchen stools. They were the variety that can be purchased retail at $8-$10. She made her fabulous buy for only $2 each. Though both the seats and rungs were well worn, and successive layers of paint applied by former owners were clearly visible, she was delighted with her purchase.

Visiting her home some time later, we saw the stools in her kitchen. They had been sanded, stripped of paint, and stained. They looked just as they would have had she purchased them new. We asked if she had done the work herself. "No", she said, "I had them done. The workman only charged me $50 for the pair." She is, even today, delighted by her purchase. She regularly informs visitors, "I bought them at auction for only $2, a fabulous buy."

She is a constant reminder to us: "Beware of 'fabulous buys' that will soak up resources beyond the potential real value of the purchase." Of course there is something to be said about the love of restoring used goods to their original beauty, no matter the cost. To her, indeed, her home is dominated by fabulous buys, well worth whatever the costs of her restorations.

A "Potty Chair" Fixation

When we preview merchandise before an auction, whenever a potty chair is found, I know it will be ours as soon as it is brought up to bid. Regardless of cost, the chair's value is almost immeasurable to my husband. He collects potty chairs. At present, we have six and this does not count the two he parted with as gifts to friends. I am not speaking of the potty chairs commonly used to train children. These are chairs that were for centuries used in bedrooms before indoor plumbing became common. You may know them as commodes. Some we have purchased are beautifully crafted, evidencing pride of workmanship performed long ago.

We have a hand-made large chair of bleached oak, intricately carved, presumably the work of, or for, the male of an earlier generation household. Another chair is part of a set, including both male's and lady's chairs, as well as a small lift-top chest. The set is closely-woven wicker, with the original silk fabric and its slightly faded flowers covering the flip-top seat of each chair. It is really quite a beautiful period set, dating to the first 15-20 years of the 20th Century.

My husband's personal favorite is a mahogany chair. Each rung in the ladder back is carved, and the legs replicate the patterns on the chair's rungs. Restoration had occurred before we bought it at auction. I covered the seat with a fabric appropriate to its present-day setting, in the sitting area of our bedroom, which is dominated by antiques.

When potty chairs are placed on the block auctioneers often make derisive comments on their use. Some auctioneers suggest alternative uses: "An interesting flower pot", "An ice chest for parties, sure to cause comment." Although none of our potty chairs is used in such ways, we know they could be. Meanwhile, should our plumbing ever go haywire – always a possibility in our 100-year-old home – we are prepared!

My husband justifies the expenditure: "The chairs can do nothing but increase in value," he says. Presumably, one day we will sell his treasured potty chairs. However, I think it more likely we will, over years, accumulate even more, and he will ever be secure in the knowledge he has ready access to an endless supply of alternatives if the bathroom fixtures fail.

Jelly, Toilet Paper, Mustard...

Anything that is used by man or beast can be sold at auction. Though most items fit into neat categories of expected auction items, some do not. You never know precisely what to expect, as an acquaintance and I found as we prepared to enter an auction.

A grocery store was going out of business. The owner consigned everything in the store to auction. Before any of the paraphernalia of the store was sold, the grocery supplies were put up for bid. The auctioneer offered each kind of product separately. Therefore, a shelf of jelly, a half-shelf of toilet paper, a row of canned vegetables, and so on, was auctioned each as a single lot. Attendees purchased 100 or more individual grocery items at a time. One bidder was particularly ambitious, as we discovered before entering the auction place.

We were attracted to a car in the parking lot with an open trunk and a man standing by it, a long list in his hand. The trunk was jam-packed with groceries, which some of us bought because of the excellent prices. The car owner was also offering other items from a list. He agreed to deliver these orders to us. It was a strange way to grocery-shop, but the prices we paid were well below retail. I bought jelly, toilet paper, mustard, and paper napkins. I was rather concerned about the age of some of the canned goods and other items, such as the toothpaste he offered, so I got into a conversation with him.

Ultimately I asked him, "About how much did you have to pay for all of the groceries you bought?" The question would be inappropriate in most sales settings, but to auction buffs this kind of question is always acceptable. He told me he paid less than $100 for everything he had purchased. The approximate retail value of the goods was $1,200.

Purchases at most auctions will average about 20-25 percent of expected retail prices, though often the bid prices are substantially less. So his purchases and resales were exceptional buys. Obviously, he could not move into another kind of parking lot, raise his trunk lid, and proceed to sell jelly and toilet paper in large quantities to passersby. But he had anticipated this. "I've already sold a good deal of them," he said. "I just called family and friends, and many purchased entire lots of some of the groceries."

It's not a situation that falls into the laps of auctiongoers often, but it suggests how some buffs can spot and take advantage of an unexpected opportunity. I had to admire the man. And certainly this incident whetted my appetite for grocery auctions. I can clear a shelf for a case of bargain jellies as fast as a sprinter can breast the finish tape.

Speaking of Clothes

One evening we made an unusual purchase, one which today we live in on a regular basis.

Many auctions have clothing for sale. Often it is found inside sealed boxes at a warehouse auction, or hung for display at the auction house or, in some instances, shown in piles on floors, yards, and in boxes. Some auctions even regularly purchase new clothes to be sold. These items are usually close-outs from a manufacturer, or have been purchased from specialty stores, or even placed on consignment by the manufacturer.

Almost always, whatever the condition of the clothing, buyers are found. Used clothing and furniture stores, second-hand stores and even some excellent antique stores purchase the clothing. New clothing often results in very strong, competitive bidding. We, like many regulars, have sometimes purchased new clothing although, as a regular policy, we have never purchased used clothing because we have no ready means for its disposal. However, we made an exception in one massive purchase.

As we entered the auction house, we saw two very long racks of clothing. Each item was covered by plastic, and had a dry cleaner's identification tag attached. The clothes were tightly bunched on the racks, and the crowd so large that no one could review the racks carefully. Still, it was an interesting lot.

The clothing was supplied by a dry cleaning establishment. When clothes are not picked up after a specified period of time, dry cleaners can dispose of them to partially recoup the cleaning charges. Here was an entire cleaner's collection, all assigned a single lot number, among the many lots of different items to be sold that evening.

Considering that most people do not send their everyday clothing to cleaners, with the exception of shirts, which did not appear to be on the racks for auction, we decided to take a chance and bid on the two racks of clothes. We won! We paid $80 for all the clothing on two racks – more than 400 hangers of clothing. Most of the bagged items had more than one hanger of clothing inside. But we didn't know what it was we had purchased.

We went home, the back of our suburban jammed full, anticipating the fun we would have investigating our purchase. What did we find? Our guess had been right on target. With only a few exceptions – some men's polyester suits – our purchase was impressive. We had sports coats, suede coats, men's and women's designer suits, and a wide variety of sweaters, jackets, blouses, and slacks. There were silk dresses, raincoats and linens. We sorted the clothing by approximate sizes and sex. We filled an entire bedroom with our $80 purchase.

Because my husband and I are each rather standard sizes, our wardrobes doubled instantly. Many of the selections we opted to keep are still worn regularly. Some of my favorite sweaters, blouses, slacks, and even suits were purchased more than four years ago. (How often does good clothing go out of style?) My husband's wardrobe includes a raincoat, sport coats, jackets, and slacks. A visiting friend took home two large boxes of clothing as a surprise for his wife.

Our savings on clothing we have *not* had to

buy since then are not quantifiable; but we know the amount would be immense. We gave a great deal of the clothing to other family members and friends. Finally, when we had given away all we could, we contacted a local charity and took the excess clean clothing to them. Our purchase extended well beyond the value of our investment.

Simply because we used common sense before considering the potential value of our purchase, we succeeded. Others at that auction could also have considered that people do not send everyday clothing to cleaners, and have won the bid. Fortunately, they did not. We have never again seen such an offering at an auction. If we do, it's ours! – within reason, of course.

Desks and Drawers

I watched as my husband made the winning bid on a pile of junk. I was convinced he was suffering from "auction fever," a subject we'll deal with later.

An auction was held in an area of an office-supply warehouse as the bitter end of a failing business. It was filled with desks and lateral files. As Fred's bid reached $70, I shuddered. We would have to move all of this heavy stuff, and then what would we do with the purchases? The contents included two wooden and one metal full-sized desks and, to my horror, unassembled metal files and shelving – enough of each to outfit several large offices.

Two days later, we returned with our trailer. Aided by several warehousemen, we packed our $70 purchase. Dusty and dirty, and exhausted from helping with the loading, I questioned my husband. "What are you planning to do with all of this stuff?" He had answers.

Several teachers he works with wanted desks for their personal use. We sold each of the three desks for $75, a profit of $155. But we still had all the unassembled shelving and files, with no storage space for our massive purchase. We donated the files to a charitable organization, which was delighted to have the wrapped, assembled piles of office necessities. They would put their handicapped workers to work assembling these things. They would sell the finished sets at their furniture outlet.

Not only did our purchase provide work and profit for the charity, it also gave us a charitable donation that was substantially more than we paid for the merchandise, as we can add in the costs of transportation. We recouped our cash investment and, with the tax write-off against our small business, added some unseen dollars to justify future purchases. Just like a "big guy" business!

Beware This Ague — Auction Fever

Auction fever is a condition much like the gambling urge that sets in when an amateur enters the premises. Suddenly the unlikely seems logical. The urge to splurge chases out horse sense. Desires never before recognized come to the fore. The ordinarily placid man or woman becomes uncharacteristically competitive. Too often, there goes the bankroll. The first thing a newcomer to auctions should guard against is catching this disease. It can be painful. Many experience it. And sometimes it overcomes even the hardened pro who, throwing caution to the winds, enters the auction for something he or she knows to be impractical, useless, or overly expensive. That thought brings me memories of the three-ton oven we bid in one day, after moving into our present house.

A Three-ton Stove

Antique homes have advantages. Three generations of a family lived in ours before we bought it, and as a result of many additions over the years, it has become spacious. Our kitchen, for example, is large, measuring 18x22 feet, providing ample space for seating and cooking. In the space used for our stove there was a fireplace, one of two that were part of the original structure. The attic still holds the brickwork of the original kitchen fireplace.

Stoves available today are lost under the large vent that replaced the lower portion of the fireplace. We found a 1940s "Crown" stove with two ovens and two broilers. It fills our needs and almost fits well into the area. Yet, in the back of our minds, we had a hankering for an old-fashioned iron stove, though certainly it would have to be modernized to substitute gas for wood or coal.

One evening at auction, we saw "the" stove. It was indeed iron. Though not refitted to gas use, it was perfect. The stove was part of a collection from a restaurant that had long since gone out of business. It not only had iron lids covering the burners; it had two ovens, and a large grill on top. Excitedly, we bid on the stove. We won! It was a case of auction fever.

After the auction, in more sober reflection, we realized the monumental task we faced in moving the stove. It weighed an estimated three tons. We told the auctioneer we would have it picked up. We were elated – until it dawned on us that we'd made a mistake. The price of our winning bid was not high, as few others had entered bids. And, even though the cost of having the stove picked up would add to the price, we had overlooked an obvious problem, one which could not be resolved without major and costly home renovation.

Our old house is built on a "pier and beam" foundation common in many parts of the South and Southwest. The flooring is built across beams driven into the ground. The house is, therefore, raised above ground by the height of the supporting beams. This is not visible from the street, but we have to consider the weight-bearing limitation of our flooring.

Our three-ton stove would require major reinforcement beneath the house and, in all likelihood, well beyond the space under the stove. To use our great discovery could cost us tens of thousands of dollars. Our stove purchase was a mistake. We could not, however, compound the mistake by investing even more in its removal to our house. We could not use it, and we should have realized that before the auction fever bug bit us.

The following day, we returned to the auction house, explained our predicament, and re-consigned the stove to the next auction. To our great relief, it sold then and, fortunately, near the price we had paid for it. So we lost only the re-consignment fee paid to the auction house. Yet the experience was galling. As auction veterans, we should have known better.

The "Perfect" Sink

Our guesthouse – a euphemism if there ever was one because it contains, not people, but materials bought at auction – holds three large crates. Within each crate nestles a beautiful Italian sink. The designs in each are hand-painted, and then porcelainized. The sinks were an unexpected find of great beauty.

We got these at a junk auction featuring hundreds of shabby sofas, chairs, dated office equipment, and a plethora of other items of no interest to us. But in a single corner of the large dirty warehouse was a pile of more than 50 crates. Each contained one of these new Italian sinks.

Finally their lot number was called. The auctioneer informed us he would sell them "to the highest bidder, with bidder choice." This meant that a bidder could take one, or if he wanted, up to fifty of the sinks, paying the winning bid price for each. We entered the bidding hoping that either we would win, or that the winner would not purchase all of the sinks. By entering the contest, we put the auctioneer on notice of our interest in buying at least one of them.

Somebody else topped the bidding at $28, but the winner chose to buy only a few of the sinks. The auctioneer then turned to others who had bid on the lot and asked each if they wanted to purchase one or more sinks at the winning price. Fortunately, we were asked first because ours had been the last bid before the final one. When we did not increase our offer, there were no others to counter his $28 offer. We quickly responded with a request for three sinks. The next bidder in line informed the auctioneer that he would take the balance of the sinks at the bid price.

Once we owned the sinks, however, we had to put them to use. And that's where our frustration came in. Our three bathrooms already have sinks, but none is fitted with the counters or cabinets that the new sinks would require. Then we discovered that all the sink hardware we own is useless for the new ones. If we ever do use them, we will need not only cabinets but hardware and plumbing fittings as well.

It has been almost a year since we bought those "treasures". We are waiting to find an auction with sink cabinets and the correct hardware. Heaven forbid we should buy them at retail. Knowing that the sink installation is his job, (I am ignorant of all plumbing matters and intend to remain so) my husband has convinced me to wait. "Certainly," he points out "we don't want to pay only $28 per sink, and then have to lay out another $150 for a cabinet and hardware for each." While I understand his pragmatic approach, I am not convinced. Those crates may still be gathering dust when we retire.

A Crib in Need

Attending a favorite auction, we found other regulars present that day and, as usual, a few new faces in attendance. Two women we had never seen came at different times, each accompanied by her husband. The two women were well along in pregnancy.

Among the items to be called at auction was an excellent "Jenny Lind" baby crib. Jenny Lind cribs seem always in demand, whether at auction or retail stores. It was obvious these newcomers would soon have need for it. They appeared not to know each other, but each had obviously seen the offered baby bed in a preview of the merchandise and coveted it.

Considering the popularity of such beds, we knew dealers in attendance would also be bidding on this one. That is exactly what happened. Bids opened at a low level. As dealers pushed the bidding price up, one of the women entered a bid. Almost immediately, the other made a counter-bid. All dealers dropped out. They would only resell the bed in their second-hand stores. Clearly, one of the women would need the item. Judging from the size of these bidders, that could be almost immediately.

Almost in silence, we watched the bidding contest between the women. Their offers went up and up. It became a contest of wills, as well as of wallets. Finally, one of the two won. Perhaps she didn't know it, but she paid more than the retail price. In fact, the loser at the auction was the winner. She could buy a new Jenny Lind crib, at retail, and save money.

Nevertheless the winning mother-to-be was thrilled by her success at bidding. So too was the audience. The auctioneer commented that the baby should be named for himself or his wife. The winner informed the fascinated audience that the baby was overdue. Indeed, if she had not left soon afterward, our ability to deliver a baby might have been tested. We all applauded the contest. It was good theater with high human interest.

But it was also an example of auction fever at its most common level. The lesson, I guess, is that if you're to throw caution out the window, do it with high drama.

But There's More to It

These examples demonstrate the kind of opportunities available and some of the pitfalls threatening the amateur attending his or her first auctions. The key lessons:

→ Review the sale items in advance;
→ Decide what you do and do not want to bid on;
→ Establish the maximum you want to pay for those items that interest you;
→ Avoid auction fever like the plague.

Knowing no more than this, you stand a good chance of coming out a winner.

Still, a more thorough understanding of the auction process will make you a far more competent and selective player in this money-saving, money-making game. Some of the terms commonly used by auctioneers, if not clearly understood, can lead to costly financial mistakes. You should learn distinctions among the kinds of auctions, which are extremely varied, particularly in and around metropolitan areas.

To avoid being stuck with shoddy merchandise, you ought to learn how and when to suspect that an auction or an auctioneer may not be fully on the level. Some auctioneers have trade tricks or stage manners that can mislead you if you're not aware of them. There are lots of other things to know that will give you the assurance you need to shop the auction route knowledgeably and therefore profitably.

Chapter Three

An Introduction to Auctions

The fear of intimidation is probably the biggest deterrent to would-be auction attendees. Some expect to be exposed to a baffling chant by the auctioneer when, in fact, most American auctions are carried out in ordinary English.

Before Fred and I became auction-addicted, we had unsatisfactory experiences and rarely made purchases. We felt confused. We lacked confidence. We were ourselves intimidated by the presence of dealers and sophisticates – and sometimes by the pace of the action. That was before we were married, when we each attended alone. Having a companion at these affairs after our marriage made a significant difference in our attitudes. We firmly believe it is a good idea, at least for the inexperienced, to take a friend or relative along because one gives the other support, and neither is likely to be embarrassed by what may seem like gaffes to an outsider.

There is a tendency to think, incorrectly, that there is something new or unique about auction-buying. Indeed for the modern retail shopper the concept may be new. But auctions have dominated nearly every major commercial activity throughout the world for hundreds of years.

Auctions have long been the medium of exchange for commodities. Images of tobacco and cattle auctions are common to the American experier 'e. What is the stock exchange, but an auction; that i , a request for a bid, acceptance of the offer, and the opportunity to buy or sell stock? In earlier generations, the auction served as the means to establish market value effectively at some point in the chain from producer to consumer for almost all products.

For most of the 20th Century, Americans have been accustomed to having wholesale and retail prices set by sellers. If "the customer is always right" in the officious claim made so often, it follows that the customer should establish the price, which is what happens at auctions. In many industries, this actually occurs at the production end of the scale from raw material to consumer.

Grain, oil, diamonds, land, futures, and many other forms of commercial trade take place in large-scale versions of retail auctions. Controlling the amount of merchandise available for bid is a well-known device to set a floor under auction prices. Witness the tactics employed by OPEC, the diamond cartel, and even the governmental price-support systems employed in such commodity fields as wheat, corn, sugar, milk, and cattle. And that of course has a strong bearing on what the ordinary citizen pays for these products. Even with these limitations, most commodity trading meets the auction standard of sellers setting asking prices and buyers making bids, with the sales usually going to the highest bidders.

Auctions at the consumer level have never fully lost popularity, even with the availability of retail stores. Australia today conducts 90 percent of its home sales by public auction. Few home-sellers there have to wait weeks or months to see if someone will meet the prices they ask. Instead, homes are put on the market, and buyers establish the selling price. And since this is done under competitive circumstances, the end result is usually satisfactory to both seller and buyer. The give-and-take that characterizes some old-world markets approaches what we experience at auctions involving groups of men and women on an individual level.

A wise Hoosier auctioneer observed to me: "Give me a start-up business with a new item to sell, and I'll quickly find the market value of the product." He added the disclaimer: "However, sometimes a product that bombs in one area will move like wildfire in another. An auction is a very fast way to find out a product's value to the public, and it beats the costs of a market survey."

The happy truth is that even the rankest amateur will find opportunities at retail auctions to establish his or her own price for something appealing. While this is a rare experience to the ordinary American shopper, it is a commonplace to those of us who have discovered the advantages of buying at auction. To many first getting their feet wet in this form of retail buying, the auction opens up a whole new world of possibilities that can make a poor family feel enriched.

Intuitively, I had acquired much of this information during 20 years in retailing, before entering the academic world. My husband worked for years as a comptroller and supply officer in the military, before he became a government property appraiser. Finally, intuition and tenacity, combined with our mutual desire to beat the system, led us into a new world: the old world of auctions for pleasure and profit.

Each day, moving from room to room in our home, Fred and I are surrounded with reminders of auctions we have attended and the memorable moments of their purchase. When friends visit, conversation often turns to acquisitions throughout our large old home. We give casual tours of the five bedrooms, three baths, and two studies, pointing out our triumphs at auction. As a daughter observes, "It's like visiting a museum, with constantly changing displays". Our combined incomes don't justify a single museum piece, yet we have them throughout the house.

Sometimes, when the things begin to overwhelm us, or a new purchase is so dominant and in need of display, we re-do rooms, even the entire house, to make use of our auction purchases. We sell left-overs for profit.

Recently, I wallpapered a bedroom. Earlier, I had papered the dining room and living room. For weekends to come, I have wallpaper for all of the other rooms in our home. Another daughter, an interior designer, accords the term "old world" to our home as it is developing.

A neighbor is also beginning work on her home, wallpapering two rooms. We still have enough wallpaper for five, or more, large homes. The cost to us? Nothing! We bought the wallpaper for $80, a price not uncommonly paid for paper for a single roll. Our neighbor bought her paper from us at $6 a double roll. She and others will purchase the balance of the paper, wiping out our costs, and we'll make a substantial profit in the bargain. We will report the costs and income on our taxes, but we also can deduct one of the rooms as our office, where business is conducted, helping to balance out the costs of our hobby with our weekly, or more frequent, visits to auctions.

Every room in our home is enhanced by a large oriental rug. Some are genuine originals; others are factory-made, contemporary style. Our "guest house" is filled with "treasures" from auctions that we sell, advertising the availability of an armoire, a lighting fixture, dishes, or merely a semi-new sofa, chair, or dining table.

Two computers sit side-by-side in our study. One was purchased new from a computer store, and cost more than $1,500. The other, a brand-new IBM clone with hard-drive and printer, cost us $600. It was purchased at auction. We have boxes of "junk" and diamonds. There is no electrical appliance we do not now have, or have had. This tip-of-the-iceberg list is a result of knowing auctions; the what, where, when, how, and why. The point is that anybody can do the same with a little experience, combined with a growing knowledge about auctions.

We began to acquire that after we married and found ourselves in need of many basic household amenities and essentials. One day we drove by an auction sign in a nearby neighborhood. We attended and were lucky. This committed us to auctions (perhaps addicted would be a more appropriate term). Now, after seven years, we have studied auctions, auctioneers, and even books on collectibles. We sometimes make mistakes, but now they are infrequent. When we pull a boner, it helps to remember that even the curators of great art museums have occasionally been hoodwinked.

Some years ago, a new auction house opened. We did make a mistake that surely was avoidable, and it may be instructive to amateurs. We were looking for the English imports advertised as the house's specialty. Two hours after the auction began, a single pub-chair was brought in front of the audience. My husband and I were in different parts of the large crowded room. The auctioneer explained that the chair was one of six. The purchase would be one, "times the money". Fred and I had spotted only one of the chairs, and we wanted it.

I bid on it thinking only the single chair was being offered, and discovered I had a competitor. I raised the bid of $13 to $20, seeking to end the prolonged dollar-at-a-time process. I won. But, as the auctioneer pronounced my winning bid "$20, times six" to the clerk, I realized my mistake. When Fred and I got together afterwards, I apologized for committing us to the purchase of six chairs for $120. Only then did I discover that he was the man bidding against me!

A lesson learned. Now either we agree to stay together, or determine in advance which of us will bid. But then, hoping to recoup our purchase price, we decided to re-consign the chairs to a later auction at the same place. This was an option for buyers written in the house catalog.

But we had not read the fine print, which would have informed us that the auction house reserves the right to determine how items will be brought up for sale. Two weeks later, when the chairs were again put up for bid, they were presented as "one money buys all". The auctioneer also fulfilled his claim, as he had not done the first time, that he would point out the flaws in the items, "as we see 'em".

Two of our chairs were damaged. Therefore, as a group of six chairs, with two broken, they sold for a total of $43. We owed the auctioneer one-third of the selling price, "to the nearest dollar," under the terms of our reconsignment agreement. We received a check in the mail for $29, on our investment of $120 plus 3 percent for credit-card financing. Even rank amateurs could see that with this kind of "success" at auctions, we would soon be broke. The mistakes were due to inattention and carelessness. The newcomer should avoid such errors at auction as most do at any other kind of sale.

An Overview of Auctions

An auctioneer friend introduces each sale he conducts with the statement, "The first bid is an offer to purchase; the second bid makes [this] an auction". Therefore, an auction is a competition between two or more potential purchasers of an item.

Competition for some items can be fierce. Auctioneers normally divorce themselves from active support of one or another bidder, but they always recognize competition and use it, when possible, to increase purchase prices. Generally, the more people in attendence at an auction, the higher the selling prices. However, the kind of people in the audience (many call it the house) can also make a difference in both the intensity of the bidding and the prices an item will reach.

When we first attended auctions, we were put off to find a substantial number of dealers in attendance. The term "dealer" fits a range of individuals who may be shopping for items for resale at flea markets, used-car/furniture/appliance stores or at other auctions, garage sales, etc. As our knowledge increased, we came to appreciate houses filled with dealers. Why? Dealers purchase for resale. They always temper the prices they pay with their knowledge of how much they can expect to resell for. They also have to consider the amount of space the item will take in their storage/sales facilities, their cashflow, and other businesslike concerns. All of that limits their bids.

On the other hand, individuals seeking to add to collections, or purchase for personal use, do not have to consider mark-up in their bids. Dealers generally do not pay as much for an item as will a private collector or purchaser, unless he or she is acting on behalf of a customer. Only then, dealers may out-bid private bidders. Now, after years at auctions, we are delighted to find a house filled with dealers. So we caution those putting their toes into the water for the first time not to allow the presence of dealers to deter them.

Even dealers with deep pockets often have to defer to private individuals. A couple we know own a very large, very posh, specialty/used-furniture store. They have a system for auction buying. The wife previews the items to be offered for sale and identifies those to be bid on, then her husband takes over the bidding.

She sets maximum amounts to offer for each item. Rarely does he exceed her limits. At some auctions, the mere presence of this couple intimidates less financially secure dealers from bidding. The couple's mark-up is higher than that of most small stores, and they have a warehouse, so they can afford to bid higher than other dealers. Nevertheless we sometimes watch the husband shake his head in amazement when private bidders enter higher bids. The differences are in the use of the items. Private bidders are buying for personal use; profit is not their motivation.

Another fact of life for amateurs: Auctions are conducted to earn income for someone. It is up to the auctioneer to see that the items sell for the best prices he can draw from the house. Auctioneers may be selling items they own as part of the auction house stock, or they may be selling items placed with the auctioneer for sale, or both. Either way, the auctioneer is in the business to make a profit.

If the items are owned by the house, the auctioneer will mentally, sometimes even formally, set a minimum price he needs to make a profit. He may have been given a minimum acceptable price by the consignor of the other goods, of which he will retain a percentage. He has to think of the total house income from any given auction sale from which to derive net earnings. The winning price for any single item for sale may not be important to the auctioneer, so long as he or she can anticipate a satisfactory amount from the auction as a whole.

Often, therefore, house-owned items sell for very low prices. This is not unlike loss-leader items sold in large retail stores, but which will be balanced by higher mark-ups on other items. This knowledge can work to the advantage of buyers who understand the values of items for which they're searching. Some merchandise may be sold at rock-bottom prices. But it is well to know what "rock-bottom" is because it may be reached rapidly in successive bids before the unaware novice hears the auctioneer's "Sold" that closes bids.

To a certain degree, there is an element of gambling in auction attendance; some advantages are always with the house. The auctioneer has an advantage because only he or she knows the profit-margin needs of the house. The auctioneer determines which items, or how many items, he or she can sell at low prices, while still running a successful business. As in Las Vegas or at the track, the best gamblers are those who know most about the subject. Acknowledging the house advantage is the beginning of auction wisdom.

Types of Auctions

Somewhere in this country, in every large metropolitan area, there is an auction under way. Sometimes in anguish I regret not being there. At other times I have no interest in going. That's because there are many types of auctions. Some are of no interest at the moment, and others never are. The newcomer needs to pick and choose from the many available. So it helps to be able to differentiate among auctions from the outset.

The following chapters help to do that. Each identifies a particular kind of auction and suggests

43

why they may – or may not – be right for your needs. A knowledge of auction types helps you to learn what to expect, how to find them, and other inside information that is probably otherwise not available to you. Keep in mind that the more you know about the subject, the better prepared you are to buy chic and buy cheap.

Chapter Four

General or Junk Auctions

You will notice few, if any, dealers advertising their sales as general or junk auctions, but you'll learn that most auction buffs think of them in those terms. That's because there's no classifying such collections. Some of us would rather go to a junk auction than to the circus.

The sale items are miscellaneous – beyond categorizing – and the premises may be so amorphous as to give the appearance of junkyards. That's not always the case, but if you attend one of these, be prepared to climb over and around mounds of materials, packed or unpacked, and sometimes covered with dust. You may also be surprised to find everything as neat and orderly as in a department store or a zoo, with the difference that all departments are usually rolled into one in an auction house, and the animals are stuffed.

Many of us look forward to such affairs because, in the midst of what appears to be chaos, we sometimes find treasures. And usually they come at ridiculously low prices. This kind of auction is, in fact, our favorite because of the element of surprise it so often affords. Regular auction attendees become accustomed to hearing "dream" stories of fabulous finds.

The owner of a used furniture store picked up a badly worn sofa at a junk auction. When she removed the dirty cushions to clean them, she felt around the sides of the sofa and found $1,200 in carefully folded bills. The original owner was untraceable, so this woman was substantially enriched.

Fred and I saw a set of Noritake china brought to bid by the auctioneer at a junk auction. He admitted there were some pieces missing, so there wasn't much interest among the attendees. We bought it for $20. Once we unpacked the crate, we found we had purchased two dated sets of this valuable china, and only five plates were missing. In time we were able to replace the missing pieces at a china specialty store, although we had to pay $50 for them. That brought the number of place settings to sixteen, in addition to the usual double serving pieces. Today, each place setting sells for at least $50, so our investment is now worth more than $800, even if resold at an auction.

A German family, long settled in the U.S., decided to unload many of its old-world treasures when moving to smaller quarters. Some of their belongings brought high prices at auction. But one piece, a rolled-up tapestry, got little attention from the audience, and we bought it for $27.50. We offered to return it when we discovered that the woman who owned it had specified that the minimum bid be set at $200, a fact the auctioneer had overlooked. She refused our offer, even though the tapestry was an original Gobelin purchased in France.

It now graces a 4x8-foot space above our fireplace mantel. It has been appraised at more than $1,200 and we figure it will ultimately be a part of our children's heritage.

Visitors to our house tend to oh-and-ah over some of the treasures it holds. That includes a grandfather clock inset with mother-of-pearl and handpainted in oriental design despite its German works and chimes; a Drexel dining room table and six chairs; an entire new bedroom set, including a queen-size bed, mattress and springs, night stand, dresser and vanity with mirror, and many other items. No set or piece was bought for more than $290.

Such finds are not as newsworthy as one man's discovery of an original copy of the Declaration of Independence beneath a framed picture picked up at a garage sale. He turned it over to the famed auction house Sotheby's in Manhattan, where it sold for $2.4 million. The point is that truly desirable merchandise of almost any variety is regularly acquired, in good condition, at junk, or general, auctions for a song.

We have found curiosity pieces, antiques, collectibles, boats, cars. We have purchased "lots" of sealed boxes and rolled rugs, never knowing what's in hand until getting them home. Sometimes we're pleased, sometimes not, but the costs are so low we can't get too disappointed.

We have supplied others with every conceivable kitchen utensil, flatware and silverware, old portraits, picture frames, gallons of paint and perfectly sound color television sets. We have taught children and friends not to buy major appliances such as washers, dryers, dishwashers, stoves, barbeque grills or microwave ovens without checking with us first. We may have them on hand. If not, we'll pick them up as bargains at junk auctions.

Many household items offered at auction are complete with manuals, and often manufacturers' guarantees still in force. Less often, guarantees are made by the auction house. Many of these businesses offer 48-hour guarantees on major appliances so the buyer has time to determine whether they work properly. If not, they can be returned for a full refund.

How do you find these events?

Perhaps the simplest way is to let your fingers wander through the yellow pages to "Auction Houses" or "Auctioneers", pick a number, and call with your questions. If auction houses are listed, they are almost certainly permanent businesses. Most will probably balk at describing their sales with the words "junk" or "general". If they say they deal in household belongings, general merchandise, or miscellaneous goods, it's a fair guess that they belong in the junk or general category.

Such permanent businesses usually have fixed schedules and locations for their auctions and make provision for you to review the items that will be up for bid in advance of the auction itself. This may, or may not, be helpful, depending upon the company's degree of orderliness in storing its goods.

In most locations auction houses or individual auctioneers use classified advertising sections of local newspapers to publicize auctions.

Major metropolitan newspapers carry a classified section entitled "Auctions". Where they do not, auctions are sometimes listed under "merchandise for sale" or other classifications. Neighborhood shoppers and weekly newspapers in some locations are prime media for auctioneers. If there is some doubt where you live, call the nearest newspaper and ask for the identity used.

General auction businesses often run simple, brief notices simply stating "Weekly/biweekly/monthly auction held on (date)", with telephone number and address. General auctions usually do not advertise the items to be offered. That's because the owner frequently is unsure what his merchandise will be. He's at the mercy of consignees or others whose deliveries probably have no relationship to advertising deadlines. Some auction houses regularly use general terms such as "household furnishings, tools, miscellaneous". The reader can assume this is a general or junk auction. You won't know what's on sale until you review the merchandise or attend the auction.

Most auctions are held on fixed schedules so that dealers and regular attendees can plan in advance. And regular attendance carries some advantages with it. Once the auction personnel become aware of your interests, they may call to give you advance notice of items to be put up for bid that they know you are interested in. They'll often do this for dealers, too. Of course it is in the house interest to encourage attendance, for the larger the audience the better the opportunity for the house to encourage bidding up prices.

This does not, however, indicate that regulars get any kind of break in the bidding. Legitimate auctioneers do not give special opportunities to any bidders, beyond perhaps extending courtesies appropriate to friends. Once the auction begins, friendship between auctioneer and bidders ceases as truly as between opposing pitchers in a baseball game. Everybody in attendance recognizes that the auction is a business and profit is the driving force behind it.

As for the excitement an auction arouses: it can run hot and cold. For a first-time viewer the esthetics may be a put-down. Every site differs, mainly in the space available for display of the items to be sold. Some appearances are pleasing; others more closely resemble an abandoned, hopelessly cluttered closet, room, garage, or even back yard. Don't walk away if this is the case. You may miss out on some impressive bargains.

The length of time an auction lasts depends mainly upon the amount of merchandise to be offered, but also upon the speed with which the auctioneer works. Auctioneers are an interesting breed with many different characteristics. We'll deal with them in a later chapter.

Some auctions may take no longer than an hour. Others may go on for three hours or more. Your interest in staying the distance is, of course, conditioned by the items you intend to bid upon. Often it is possible to get an idea of the order in which they will come up for bid by reading a formal schedule provided by the house, or by asking the auctioneer in advance of the action. On many an occasion we have left for an hour or so to do other things and returned in time to make our bids on items we have selected in advance.

Chapter Five

Warehouse Auctions

$\mathbf{A}$uctions held by storage warehouses tend to be more orderly than general auctions, but the zing of surprise is often greater – and for a good reason. That is because much of the bidding is on "blind" items, usually unopened boxes or crates. And because they are unopened, and the value of the contents have to be guessed at, the winning bids are usually modest.

It should be understood that, although some general, or junk, auctions are held in warehouses, the storage warehouse auctions are distinctive. Warehouses store goods for a fee, the amount of which is partially dependent upon the length of time in storage. When the time is up and the fee unpaid, storage warehouses are entitled to take ownership of what appears to be abandoned goods, and to resell them. This is the basis for warehouse auctions.

The source of such goods and the cause of their coming up at auction may vary greatly. Companies and people alike tend to put into storage the goods they can't accomodate on their premises, but don't want to dispose of. Then the owners may move away, die, lose interest, or simply forget the items in storage, leaving the warehouse owners without income from the space occupied. Some warehouse goods may be damaged in moving. The insurance pays the owner, and the warehouse retains the damaged goods. No matter the source, the warehouse ownership is established firmly by state or federal law, so auction bidders need not worry about the legality of their purchases.

Many items at warehouse auctions are open to inspection. Most owners don't pack furniture or other large belongings. We have seen regular furniture, interspersed with kayaks, mooseheads, automobile engines, and other such things, displayed in advance of the auction.We have purchased rugs, desks, a child's high chair and a blackboard. But the items that intrigue us and many other auction regulars are the unopened boxes, which are always at least partially mysteries.

Whether the warehouse is huge or modest in size, the boxes are usually piled up, one atop the other. Many are labeled by the owners: "Kitchen", "Glassware", "Books", "Bedroom", etc. But does "Glassware" mean jelly glasses or Steuben crystal? Do "Books" mean *Playboy* magazines, or leatherbound first editions?

Certainly the owners knew what the labels meant when they wrote them. But the storage house, the auctioneers, and the auction attendees do not. Hence the fun! Fun, tempered with caution. If you are tempted to bid, you must remember that you're buying a pig in a poke. Yet there are clues to note and interpret.

We have invested sometimes substantial but usually modest sums in purchasing such alluring boxes. The openings always bring a surprise. We have shared elation with others as they've looked into their surprise packages. We have also felt disgust at what some owner saw fit to pack into boxes with and without identifying labels. Fortunately, most such surprises are pleasurable.

We picked up a large box labeled "clothing" for under $10 and discovered we owned four sets of brand new skiing outfits, including jackets, leggings, boots, hoods and mittens. Although we do not ski, we do fish. Two of the sets fit us perfectly. Casting our lines into the Gulf of Mexico on cold nights or days, we can be seen fashionably attired in our $2.50 matching sets of cold-weather gear. A daughter took her first ski trip outfitted with the other two sets.

One clue we look for is the lot number on a visible item offered to bid that may be foreign, or elegant, or well-kept. If that same number is borne on a closed box, indicating the same ownership, we often bid on the box. This is not an infallible clue, but it works most of the time for us and for others.

Another clue is the weight of the box, if it can be reached and you can move it. Heavy boxes often contain books, kitchen appliances, even engines. By contrast, lightweight boxes can mean treasures stowed carefully in packing material, most commonly paper or styrofoam. The fullness of boxes can often be identified. Densely packed boxes may point to clothing, linens, or other malleable materials. If the box bulges without rattling, it is probably jammed with fabric of some sort.

We were bidding for a box one day against an acquaintance but, when the price neared $50, we backed off, and he won it. We accompanied him as he hauled the box to his car and opened it. He had purchased an entire set of crystal glassware for under $50. Each piece of the more than 100 in the box would have sold for more than the entire purchase price.

You can find such auctions wherever in your vicinity there is a moving company with a warehouse. Some are big enough to justify auctions at regular intervals. Others may hold them intermittently, as they gradually accumulate unclaimed goods. Such sales are often advertised in much the same way as general auctions. Watch the classified ad sections. If you don't find an ad after a reasonable time of screening, telephone the warehouse and find out what their procedures are.

This is one form of sale where the price is almost always right.

Chapter Six

Antique Auctions

Beware of the word "antique". It is one of the more flexible nouns in the English vocabulary. As a rule, it means whatever is in the mind of the user, and that may be a mystery to you. Nevertheless, antique auctions are among the most commonplace, and you are as likely to find them out in the country as in metropolises.

There are precise definitions of antiques. Dictionaries tell us that the word refers to things that belong to the past, or date from an early period of time and thus are not modern. That's pretty vague. One definition given by the Random House Dictionary is: "any work of art, piece of furniture, decorative object, or the like, created or produced in a former period, usually over 100 years ago..." It's not everyone who uses dictionary definitions and, for some, the word antique is abused freely to justify high prices. If your knowledge of antiques is slight, don't hesitate to question the auctioneer or other seller to find out how he or she is using the word.

To an auction house a piece of furniture described as a "genuine antique" usually means that it was produced sometime before the turn of the century. On the other hand, a painting described as "primitive" may or may not be an antique. It may refer to the art style, as in Grandma Moses's works. It is up to you to make the distinction when something described as "primitive" comes up for bid.

Such things as porcelain, pottery, dishes and other home decorative items may be considered antiques if they predate the Twentieth Century. But they can fall short of this distinction and still be old enough and rare enough to justify buying and selling as if they were genuine antiques. However the auction house describes them, you have to determine whether they are worth the premium that genuine antique prices carry.

Other antiques may not be very old, at least relative to the items identified above. An antique may be genuine when associated with the earliest period the item could have been created or manufactured. Obviously, a television set cannot be over 100 years old. There were no television sets a century ago. An antique television set may be only 50 years old, considering that television came into general circulation in the 1940s. A 40-year old television set is an antique. An auction house can say much the same about other modern devices, such as cars, office machinery, computers and the like.

Some auction houses make distinctions between "antiques", "period pieces", and "collectibles". But the distinctions are muddied. Period pieces may be "genuine antiques" – but not all antiques are period pieces. Experts and auctioneers know the differences. However, whether auctioneers make the distinction when calling the auction depends on personal style, knowledge of their audience, or even their honesty.

A "period piece" is a common term used by auctioneers to describe an item that was produced during a particular era. Usually the era's identification is left to the bidders. For example, "depression glass" items can be identified as period pieces. The glass was originally manufactured and sold during the 1930s – hence the name. "Art deco" furniture, paintings, and decorative items are often identified as period pieces. But, because art deco items were created in their original (not reproduction) form during the 1920s and '30s, they are never antiques. They are period pieces.

Novices at auctions often assume either that the "period piece" identifies a genuine antique, or they confuse "art deco" with "art nouveau", a style of the late 19th and early 20th Centuries. The latter may be not only a period piece, but also a genuine antique.

"Collectibles" comprise a category that is not necessarily tied to an era. They may or may not be antique. "Elvis" plates are collectibles, as are stamps, newspapers, salt and pepper sets, and any items that have acquired popular appeal. Some collectibles may be antique – a genuine suit of armor, for example – though they are usually very costly. Some collectibles are even "period pieces", depending on the auctioneer's identification system. Bottles, for instance, are often collectibles. Antique bottles are still collectibles, but they also are very old; hence their value is often quite high. Perhaps, when I am referring to bottles, I should explain that I have something of a bias that stems back to the very earliest years of my life.

An Experience with Collectibles.

Most everybody has a sensory touchstone that, when tapped, brings back a flood of childhood memories. Mine happens to be Avon bottles, and the scents and sights that go with them. My mother was an Avon lady for 35 years. Her work filled our house with the smells and sights of Avon perfumes and related products. She enlisted my sister and me as general assistants and deliverers. As a girl, I learned to loathe Avon. As a woman, I am filled with sentimental memories of youth whenever I smell the perfume or see the items associated with that era of Avon activity.

When I was a child in the 1940s, I didn't admire the beauty of the prizes my mother won for her sales work. She often received, for example, Avon plates which she kept through the years. Nor did I even dimly appreciate the variety of bottles holding the perfume she sold. One day not long ago she mentioned the plates on the phone and asked, "Would you like to have them?" I had forgotten the plates, but suddenly they seemed the most important things in the world. Now their beauty covers an entire wall of our kitchen. That reminded me of the Avon bottles, which she had not saved. We began to look for them at auctions. Periodically we purchased one or two.

Then, one day, we chanced into a new auction house. Displayed under lights of a gleaming showcase were a myriad of Avon bottles. They had been consigned to the house by a retired Avon lady now in her eighties, who *had* compiled a collection. How could I acquire these collectibles?

The auction house owner told us she would offer each piece for bid separately. This promised to be a a long drawn-out process. We left to do other things and returned just in time for the calling of the lots. By then most other attendees had left. We won each bid on the individual pieces. I was determined to acquire the entire collection, even if it meant staying all night.

But there were many bottles and few bidders. After a while, the auctioneer asked the owner of the house, "Should we put it all together and sell them as a single lot?" The owner agreed and we knew we'd win this as we had the others. Soon we were the possessors of all the remaining bottless – for only $24.

It is this kind of sentiment and determination that often characterizes bidders dedicated to their collectibles. The Avon bottles and plates are now part of our estate. To me, they are priceless because of the memories they evoke. Some day, I hope, they will be reminders to my children of the love and industry that drove their grandmother to contribute hugely to the comfort and education of her two daughters.

The Importance of Words

Some auctioneers are indiscriminate in their use of these descriptive terms. They usually know their audience contains both novices and those who are well aware of the differences in terms. But if a novice bids up a price on an item, assuming "antique" is the real meaning of either "period piece" or "collectible", the auctioneer stands to gain from this ignorance. But sophisticates in the audience may shake their heads in dismay at the auctioneer's careless use of any such terms.

At a recent auction, we joined the head-shaking, as the auctioneer identified lot after lot as "antique." She, a rare woman auctioneer, means simply that the item is old; and in her terms "old" refers to anything dating back more than 20 years. Some of the items she offers can honestly be described as "period pieces" or "collectibles" but the word "antique" flows from her head to tongue with the ease of her skill at calling the auction. Novices too often make the assumption she is really identifying a valuable piece. Accordingly, they bid high, and often discover later that they have over-paid.

Costs for items at antique auctions vary, depending on the source of supply, the rarity of the item, the sophistication of the audience, and, yes, even the prestige of the auction house. The market value is also affected by the condition of the sale item. We have known dealers to purchase excellent antiques, period pieces, or collectibles at a regional or local auction, and immediately turn them over to auction at a very prestigious auction house, such as Christie's. Profit is almost always assured; the market at the latter house is regularly attuned to paying higher prices.

Wear and damage to furniture is not necessarily valued in antiques, as some believe. Generally, the better the preservation quality of the piece, the higher the price that will be bid. Still, some pieces wear to beauty. The fine lines of age, associated with some porcelain, for instance, may add to its value.

We often carry a handbook of antiques, furniture, pottery, or whatever, with us – after we have previewed the items to be offered at auction. We then can gauge approximate prices to be expected and bid accordingly. This doesn't always work because sometimes a bidder wants a particular antique at any price. Yet this is a good practice for the novice. It assures he or she doesn't go too far astray in bidding.

Not all items offered at an antique auction are expensive. Supply and demand affect even the antique market, and prices will often vary according to audience knowledge or desires. Several years ago we purchased an antique armoire. Its wood is in perfect condition, the mirror is beveled, and all the other qualities of antique furniture exist. However, the auction house had brought a large shipment from England. There were many similar armoires available in the collection, the audience was relatively small, and we were able to purchase our beautiful armoire for only $125. In fact, we purchased two, and sold one at a profit of almost $200.

Our Parlor Set

Years ago, if someone had told me I would own a full parlor set, I'd have found the idea absurd. That was before we began to admire antiques.

One evening we spotted a broken-down set as we previewed the auction's merchandise. The stuffings were falling on the floor, the silk tufted covers were in shambles. The springs of three chairs and the love seat were barely hanging in place. The set was dust-covered, unloved by anyone. But we recognized it as Eastlake. Putting it in good shape would be lots of work, take plenty of our time, and we'd have to buy new fabric and other items. We had our doubts and so, apparently, did most others at the auction.

We purchased the set for $300 and decided to tackle the restoration ourselves. The beautiful old wood, carving intact, required nothing more than polishing to return its luster. We removed the unuseable silk upholstry, retaining button tufts for later use, and removed the straw stuffing. Inside a corner of the love seat we found a packing envelope. The 1910 owner had thoughtfully provided four of the eight buttons from the set. After searching hard, we found a store that had matching buttons, and we bought enough so that future owners might have more if needed.

Over the years we have accumulated other beautiful antiques from the same period as well as some equally old oriental chests. Could we combine the two styles and achieve a look satisfactory to our tastes? We did. Selecting a beautiful cotton fabric that coordinated with the oriental and turn-of-the-century furnishings, we covered each piece. In time we redid the rest of the room to create a designer showplace. The living room and its adjacent dining room have become our pride and joy. And the set we purchased for $300 has been appraised at $2,500 to $3,000.

Don't Be Fooled by Reproductions

A particular bugaboo in antique auctions is the "reproduction". A reproduction is not an antique. It is, instead, an item that has been created to look like an antique. Sometimes this is done so well that the reproduction is indiscernible from the original. Antique reproduction is a legitimate business, but dishonest sellers sometimes try to pass off the copy as the original. This is a con that the amateur must guard against.

We have been on hand to observe a certain woman dealer make what appear to be serious mistakes. We and other regulars have wondered how she stays in business despite the ill-advised antique purchases she so regularly makes. Nothing wrong with the auctioneer. He always advises, "This is a reproduction". I watched as she out-bid a private bidder with a $130 offer for an item that can be purchased in a chain shop for no more than $79. It remains a mystery why an experienced dealer could be out-foxed – unless, of course, there is something questionable about her business.

Our advice to auction novices is: Attend at least one auction but, unless you are skilled at identifying antiques, do not attempt to purchase unless you just like the piece, or, as occurred in our experience with the armoires, the price fits into a budget. The competition for particular pieces may be very intense. Antique dealers frequently patronize antique auctions, and they do know what it is they are viewing. But if you are not in that position, be extremely cautious.

Chapter Seven

Auto Auctions

If you have never bought a vehicle except through a dealer, the idea of an auto auction may seem odd to you. Yet the sale of automobiles – as of trucks, vans, motorcycles, boats and other vehicles – is commonplace throughout the nation. With few exceptions, the items put up for bid are used rather than new. Yet the same conditions that often provide general merchandise at true bargain prices apply to this category as well. But there are some yellow lights for the newcomer to this game, and we'll get to them.

Early on, in our auction experience, Fred and I saw one of the ugliest vans in existence sitting on the lot. It had been hand-painted orange, with erratically placed green stripes. The van, a Dodge Sportsman, had a gutted interior, save for the driver and passenger seats. But the engine, tires, and drive-train sounded and appeared in good shape. As we were beginning to think of finding a van to transport our increasingly frequent large purchases at auctions, we decided to bid on the monstrosity.

Others seemed appalled by the van's appearance. Maybe there were only a few dealers present, or no one wanted to park the orange-green ugly on their property. We purchased the 5-year-old van for $400. Two days later we sold it for $900. A friend with a perverse sense of humor wanted to park it on his employer's parking lot. He also took delight in picking up first-time dates in the "ugly," observing that her response was a measure of the new date's character. He drove the van for two years, until one day it collapsed while he was visiting a nearby city. He abandoned the van, and surely one day someone purchased the monstrosity at a sheriff's auto auction sale.

In 1990, a good deal wiser about auctions, we purchased a 1988 Renault. It was in perfect mechanical and body condition, but both the heating and air-conditioning systems were defective. We knew this at the time of purchase because the auctioneer informed the house of the problem. It was up to us to listen to the motor and inspect the body condition prior to the opening bids. We paid $3,000 for our purchase and added slightly more than $500 to repair the heating/cooling system. We had a 2-year-old car, with a total investment of $3,500. Not the best of our buys, but in my daily drives to work at the university, it serves me well.

A friend purchased a 1986 Lincoln Continental, in need of a paint job and with more than 150,000 miles on the speedometer, for $1,200. After painting and an engine overhaul, the car's total cost was under $3,000 – a "blue-book" bargain. The blue-book is a dealer's tool to evaluate prices on recent cars. It lists the prevailing prices for most makes and models, including such variations in condition as mint, good, poor.

Nearly every large city and many suburbs have auto auctions weekly or more often. The sources of the cars are many, and the sponsors of the auctions may be private or public.

Most commonly, private auctions are conducted on an auto dealer's premises. The dealer may be working with a cooperative of used-car and new-car dealers. The auction house may instead be privately owned, and seeks consignments from individuals, retail auto dealers, or even government surplus sources.

Most of the 3,000+ counties undertake these auctions, which are often labeled "Sheriff's Sales". Most Sheriff's Sales/Auctions are not, however, exclusively auctions of automobiles or other vehicles. These sales are a means of unloading used government property, items that have been abandoned or forfeited, or stuff that takes too much storage space.

Included may be confiscated properties obtained from a variety of civil or criminal actions, unclaimed lost items, contraband, etc. Expect to find almost anything imaginable – cars, RVs, and boats; desks, bookcases, chairs, books, and office machinery. But the big drawing-cards are almost always used vehicles because they are widely in demand and often represent magnificent bargains.

Other government auctions offer motor vehicles and, in addition, many sold by freelance auctioneers are acquired directly from governmental agencies. Post office, police, and other departments that are users of cars or trucks in quantity offset some of the price of purchasing replacements by auctioning off the old. They normally have a lot of miles, and, in the case of police cars, may have been used roughly. Where there are lakes and water patrols, boats may regularly appear in such "auto" auctions, as may motor homes and other vehicles.

An out-of-work neighbor purchased a city public-service van, with all of the doors and compartments associated with such a truck. Our neighbor is a good back-yard mechanic, and in a short time he had it working well, painted a sign on the door, and went to work as a freelance pick-up and delivery man. He paid for the van, and earned income until he later found a job in his field. His teenage son drove the city public service van until his graduation.

Other auto auction sources include bank and finance company repossessions and company fleet cars. Thus, dealers, private individuals, governments, banks, finance companies, and large corporations all supply vehicles for repurchase at auto auctions. The buys can be good. They can also be expensive losses. If you are a novice, at auctions or at assessing the value of vehicles, bring a knowledgeable friend with you.

Attending an auto auction can be an experience well worth the visit, both for purchasing – with some strict limitations – and for learning more about auctions.

Almost all auction houses, no matter the nature of the merchandise, require payment in cash or by pre-approved check when you pick up your purchase. At auto auctions it is not uncommon that either cash or cashier's check in a substantial amount is required at the time of registration. Your deposit will be applied to the purchase price, or will be refunded at the end of the auction. The deposit is assurance to the house that the buyer has financially committed himself or herself to a major portion of the winning bid price. Financing the balance can also be arranged, usually at the auction itself.

The range of quality of cars, trucks, vans, buses, even recreational vehicles and boats, is as diverse as is the quality and quantity of items found in most other types of auctions. Each auto auction has a tow-truck on site for pulling non-working cars onto the auction block. The "block" is normally merely a cement slab, sometimes under cover and other times out in the open. The very presence of a tow-truck is a constant reminder of the variety of vehicle qualities found at this type of auction.

Regular attendees run the gamut: used-car dealers, seeking to purchase bargains for their car lots; private buyers like you, seeking a vehicle for personal use; back-yard mechanics who will repair and resell the autos.

No auto auction we have ever attended has misrepresented the merchandise. It has always been offered "as you see it". Buyers are thus forewarned that they are responsible for previewing the vehicle and evaluating its worth.

It is important to listen closely to the auctioneer as he opens a bid because that's when he sets forth the conditions of sale, letting you know precisely what you are committing yourself to – if you bid. Sometimes these conditions are also spelled out in the catalog. In either case, pay attention.

My young daughter Julie and her husband Bob, New York City residents, had never attended an auction, but they had seen our bargains and heard us talking about auto auctions. They decided to attend one when they needed a second car. As we had advised, they took along a cashier's check for $2,000, which, if it wasn't enough to cover the cost of the car they needed, would at least be a good down payment.

Arriving late at the auction house, they saw an obviously expensive car slowly rotating on a turntable and heard the auctioneer call, "Sold, 75". He identified the winning bidder's number. That sounded good. They hurried to the registration table, signed in and, with bid card in hand, worked their way to the front of the crowd, just as the auctioneer began to call for bids on what he termed "the small burgundy-colored" car.

Bidding began with "25", and Bob jumped into the contest because they both found the car racy and attractive. At "43" Bob dropped out of the bidding. Julie tried to get him back in, but he was steadfast because they were determined not to spend more than about $4,000. The bidding stopped at "45", and the car went to a competing bidder. A man standing next to Bob leaned over and told him, "You should have stayed in...$45,000 is a steal on that car".

Only then did they realize that the bids they had made were for thousands of dollars rather than hundreds. They couldn't possibly have paid for the car if they had won it. At least it would have been a terrible embarrassment and only because, as neophytes to auctions and ignoramuses about autos, they didn't really know what they were doing. It is always necessary to listen to the auctioneer closely, and it helps if you read the catalog (when there is one) carefully before jumping into the action.

More Words of Caution

A repeated word of caution is appropriate here. Although bargains are often available, you can get scorched if you do not know how to evaluate a potential purchase intelligently. Don't go by looks alone. If you haven't the knowledge to judge a used car's quality, consult with someone who does before committing yourself. And listen carefully to the condition of sale announced by the auctioneer.

Generally, new-car dealers do not keep trade-in cars that are more than three-to-five-years old. They turn over the older models to auto auction houses, which retain a commission on the winning bidders' purchase prices. These cars are not necessarily good buys, even if the original owners were given generous credit for them, and if they are offered as "steals". Again, it's up to you to know what's in that poke you're offering good money for.

As at any similar selling action, auction fever can strike with little or no warning, and you have to guard against falling victim to it. I write this from personal experience.

Months earlier we had purchased, sight unseen, a dozen acres of wild land in the mountainous country of West Texas. We soon discovered it had few amenities, including decent roads. Getting around was a problem. Now, attending an auction, Fred spotted a motorcycle. Never mind that neither of us had ever driven one or, only as teenagers, had ridden one. Never mind that he didn't talk it over with me. He bid on it.

There wasn't much competition, and we soon found ourselves the owners of a Kawasaki 175 in excellent condition, purchased for only $90. I assumed he was getting the bike to resell it. Then he told me his purpose was to use the motorcycle to traverse our rough property and run errands more handily than in the car. The thought hardly sent a thrill of elation through me, but I agreed to go along with his plan.

He shakily drove this unfamiliar contraption home from the auction house as I, terrified, followed in the car. The following morning I climbed into the passenger seat as Fred took the handlebars for a drive down the street. Rarely have I ever been so frightened. The thought of riding on this thing, let alone driving it in bumpy passage on up-and-down unpaved country roads, was almost beyond credence. I didn't want to be a poor sport, but neither did I want the peril.

Fortunately for the stability of our marriage, a rescuer appeared at our door. It was our grown son who had always wanted, but never had, a motorcycle. Fred was having his own doubts about roaring around the woods on our new machine. He permitted himself to be sold on the idea of selling it to our son for a small profit.

He, in turn, wanted the motorcycle so he and his teenage son could run errands. But he figured without his wife's reaction, which was identical to mine. In the end, our son traded the Kawasaki, even steven, for another car. No money changed hands. But the car was valued at $800-$1,000. So the $90 purchase returned $10 profit to us and at least $700 to our son. Not bad for a few days' trading. It's one of the few happy endings to an auction fever blunder.

Despite this pot of gold at the end of the rainbow, I feel it necessary to repeat a few rules the novice should observe when deciding to attend an auto auction:

→ Go the first time to learn rather than buy;
→ When you've got bidding in mind and know little about motor vehicles, take a knowledgeable friend along;
→ Read the catalog and listen closely to the auctioneer so you understand the ground rules;
→ Remember that you'll be asked for a substantial deposit to be allowed in the bidding;
→ Guard against the rush of impetuosity known to sophisticates as auction fever.

Chapter Eight

Estate Sales

At first, there is something ghoulish about attending an auction on the site of an estate whose owner has died. On our first occasion, we found it was a deteriorated property. The house was decrepit. Floors tilted in need of foundation repair; wallpaper drooped from water damage through a leaky roof; smoke stains climbed toward ceilings where faulty space heaters were used. One could envisage the last lonely days of the elderly inhabitant as he wandered the rooms, mourning the death of his wife months earlier.

Hundreds of the curious drawn to the auction wandered from room to room, viewing contents emptied from closets into boxes labeled "linens", "pots and pans", "clothing", and "miscellaneous". An accumulation of a lifetime was on display. The old home's interior looked as if it had regurgitated its insides, and the public was reviewing its sickness. It was, in short, depressing.

Soon the auctioneer would offer the deceased owner's belongings for sale. There were no real treasures, but there would be buyers. Many in attendance decided to leave before the sale began, and so did we. It wasn't a question of whether we'd find anything useful, but rather a profound sadness to feel the meanness with which a family's life had come to a close, all their belongings exhibited and offered for sale to curious strangers. I had never experienced such overwhelming empathy.

Before departing, I sat on the crumbling side-entrance steps to the house. The steps tilted, their foundation weakened by years of slipshod care. A relief auctioneer sat down next to me. We spoke of the shabbiness of the home and I expressed my sorrow over the need for the auction. He said many people felt the same way and then posed a question: "If you were to die with no heirs and someone came to catalog all of your home's contents, including everything in your drawers, closets and cupboard, do you think most strangers would appreciate these things that you may consider treasures?"

That's when I realized that few homes, including ours, would stand up well to scrutiny by collectors, dealers and neighbors, not to mention strangers. On the other hand, those who found something worthy of buying would benefit from the acquisition; and whoever disposed of the estate would also gain from the sale. My sadness diminished. I remembered that estate auctions, like all others, are business transactions for those involved. So much for injecting one's own sentiments willy-nilly into a situation that apparently is satisfactory to those whose familial emotions have been faced and overcome.

Still, there is a fascination in tramping through the rooms and halls of an estate of those who lived well. It is easy to catch some essence of how lives were spent in a nice house with good furnishings and good vibes. It is one thing to get caught in the sorrow of a shabby home, though goodness knows it might have been overflowing with love, joy, and faith. It is quite another to sense family life in more prosperous surroundings, for the imagination is less likely to endow it with hopelessness.

Still, the auctioneer's question caused me to look with new vision at our growing accumulation of items bought at auction. I have to wonder if some day a stranger will look at a pile of hats removed from their wall display and envision my wearing them as they make their purchase. I wonder if each room's oriental rug, unvacuumed and rolled for inspection, will tempt a purchaser. Will well-used pots and pans, some with broken handles and un-cleanable bottoms, be cause for someone's sadness? Could my lingerie drawer, tumbled into a box la-beled "Clothing", serve well some secondhand store buyer? Will a box of ugly ties purchased for a collec-tor friend be mistaken for my husband's? Can any ordinary home stand objective investigation by ca-sual buyers?

Such thoughts aside, the novice considering attending an estate sale will want to think about some of the special appeals of this category of auc-tion. Usually an estate auction offers items beyond the variety available at general auctions.

We have purchased an almost new, appar-ently rarely used, Model-A Ford tool set for $3. (The car had long since disappeared.) We purchased an old wooden bed frame with built-in springs, circa 1920, and the auctioneer threw in its unwashed coverlet. The cost: $22.50.

I wear a Bulova watch exactly like the one my mother had when I was a small girl. The watch was in a "contents unknown" box my husband purchased because he had spotted some World War II military patches such as a friend collects. He paid $12.50. While investigating the contents of the box, we found the working watch, as well as several other pieces of 1930s costume jewelry.

Estates of the well-off or wealthy often contain true valuables. They may include antiques, heirlooms, original paintings and other *objets d'art*; rare books, period costumes, valuable letters or manuscripts; expensive vehicles, machinery and tool collections, or other items that could be of particular use to you. Moreover, people building or remodeling their own homes can sometimes find estate auctions in which the structure itself, or parts of it, can be bought. I know people who have bid in such things as mantels, stair rails, kitchen cabinets, bathroom accessories, bay windows, and even entire houses.

Unfortunately, many people who have never attended an estate auction associate such an event with either the ultra-rich or the hard-nosed bargain-hunters. In fact, most estate auctions are not the exclusive grounds for either. Some offer opportunities to find desirable household belongings or fixtures that rarely show up at other types of auctions. I have in mind a neighbor whose hobby is wood-working. When he acquired a new house, he bought most of the furniture for it at estate auctions because he admires the workmanship and quality of materials in older furniture much more than in new.

But there are many variations of the estate auction, some of which may mislead novices into unanticipated traps, particularly if they are romantics. An auctioneer or other sponsor of a sale rents a house, often an old and impressive building. He advertises an "estate auction", expecting novices to assume that the items in the house were part of its contents. The reality? The items for sale have been brought in, acquired by the auctioneer by much the same means to gather merchandise for junk auctions.

We know a woman who acquires old dolls wherever she can find them. She repairs the dolls and their clothing and packs them, when she can, in the original boxes, which increase their value. Then she puts them to auction in rented house "estate sales", rather than selling them from her home, or at garage or flea market sales, where the dolls would go for much lower prices. That's because newcomers to the auction scene place a higher value on items they believe to have been the property of deceased homeowners.

Another switch on the same practice: some auctioneers scan newspaper ads and obituaries to find sources of goods. They are seeking to purchase items or entire households from heirs, divorcing families, or even families moving away or to smaller homes. These may be what you buy from a rented home auction, rather than the property of the home's owner.

Auction houses often hold "estate sales" on their own properties. Commonly the merchandise is collected from a number of estates, or from non-estate sources. Many times there is no mention that the items offered are the auctioneers' or consignees' collections from multiple sources.

This may or may not be deceptive to auction attendees, many of whom don't care about the source of the goods that appeal to them. But others do and can feel bitter disappointment if they learn after purchase that they've been misled as to the origin, whether purposely or not.

Owners of auction houses have to be realistic from a business standpoint, and many estates are simply not worth an individual sale. Moreover, what may be saleable in one area may prove to be a dog in another. One auctioneer observed, "Oak furniture, regardless of age, sells well in Texas. I can't give it away in New York. There I need mahogany – not a popular wood to most Texans. In New York, a mahogany church pew will sell for $1,200 to $1,500. In Texas, the same item will sell for $300 to $500."

Indeed, some bidders in a region may make several such purchases and pay to travel elsewhere to resell them at a higher price. The reverse is also true. An individual wanting a mahogany church pew may save far more than the cost of the trip to another locale to make the purchase. Of course, no one goes to such trouble unless the value is high.

For some reason, there are many men and women who are willing to pay more for any given object bought at an estate sale than at another kind of auction. Some auction houses take advantage of this by using twists in advertising or marketing. It is not my purpose to condemn this, for the tactics are not peculiar to the auction business. But I do feel it necessary to call such matters to the attention of those who are about to experience auction buying for the first time. As in all retailing, the word is: Buyer beware.

The Gift of a Home

Often, of course, the house itself is sold, separately from its contents. And when it is bid in by an individual, rather than a real estate dealer, those in attendance may feel a distinct emotional atmosphere as the auction proceeds.

This occurred one Sunday afternoon when we attended a true estate sale in a nearby city. It was a lovely, large 1940s home. Cupboards full of personal and household belongings were sold to the highest bidders, closet contents went as single lots. Furniture, pictures, tapestries, and other household goods were in abundance. Advertising for the sale drew a huge audience from miles around, because the contents of the house included treasures collected around the world by the deceased owner, who had been a retired military officer.

The home was to be put on the block promptly at 3:00 p.m. regardless of the progress of bidding on the contents. A middle-aged gentleman arrived ahead of time for that event. He sat near us on the well-shaded lawn and said he intended to buy the house for his parents. By 3:45 the home was sold for $125,000, well below the appraised value. He was the winner. After paying (by check!), he departed.

As the disposal of the contents neared its end, he reappeared, bringing an elderly couple with him, obviously pleased with his deed and expecting, we conjectured, to find his parents elated and grateful. But we heard the old man tell his son that the home was too large. Then we eavesdropped as a loving debate took place between the son and his parents. Clearly, his mother and father were touched by their

79

son's generosity. Just as clearly, they didn't want to leave their present home. I heard the mother say, "We will move if you insist, but we're very comfortable where we are". That seemed a downbeat coda to a well-intentioned creative act.

The auctioneer told us later the conclusion of the story which, I am pleased to report, had a happy ending. This auctioneer was a good businessman. He had taken back-up bids on the house, a procedure well-known in the real estate business. This procedure allowed him to go back to the next-highest bidders in the order of their offers. The assumption is that the winner might – for one reason or another, usually lack of financing – be unable to follow through on his offer. In this case, he did not press the winner, as he might have, to force a sale, nor did he charge a fee for having to search for another purchaser, a common practice. Instead, he simply offered the house to the first back-up bidder, who agreed to buy it at the final bid price.

This considerate auctioneer won our further respect for another act at the same sale. A well-thumbed family bible was on display. It caught the interest of several potential buyers. One asked the auctioneer if the bible was to be auctioned. "No," he said, "I don't auction bibles. I just can't bring myself to do it. But if you who are interested want to get together and decide who will be the purchaser and at what price, I'll let you have it." And so he did.

Some Estate Auctions Are Off-Premises

Some estate auctions, of course, are not conducted on the premises at all; the items for sale are carted off to an auction house. But if these are expensive, or if they come from a well-known or wealthy family or individual, they are usually advertised as estate, rather than general, auctions.

You will probably remember reading or hearing about the sale of, for example, the slippers worn by Judy Garland in the Wizard of Oz; the belongings of the noted writer Alex Haley who made millions but died in debt; memorabilia attributed to singer Elvis Presley, and others. And who can forget the rage for "collectibles" during the 1980s, when famous auction houses like Christie's and Sotheby, were demanding – and getting – scores of millions for classic pieces of art? Many, though by no means all, came from estates.

Estate auctions, like most others, attract dealers in antiques, used furniture and clothing, autos, art, and other goods. You may have to compete with them in the bidding for something that appeals to you, so it's a good idea to bone up in advance on the means of recognizing the worth to you of whatever you find appealing when previewing the offerings. But keep in mind that you have one big advantage over those dealers: You don't have to take a retail markup into consideration when arriving at your maximum bid price.

Chapter Nine

Celebrity/Charity Auctions

Y ou'll have your own definition of a celebrity. For auction purposes it is anyone whose name creates enough interest among the public to draw an audience with disposable income. That can be a star of the movies, rock music, television, sports, drama, literature, or any other brand of highly visible activity; or it can be the village mayor, a local war hero, or a business leader known for philanthropy or community works.

Sometimes celebrities are even "sold". We know of an obstetrician/gynecologist who was voted one of the city's most eligible bachelors. Charity organizers regularly laid siege to "put him on the block". He has been heard to brag to his office staff, "I brought the highest price for a date". This may be great stuff for the winning women bidders, but finally he had had enough. "Given the quality of the evening," he complained after one auction, "I paid the price. Never again!"

The celebrity angle is a gimmick. It is frequently used in an auction sale to raise money for charity or another worthy cause. In such cases the celebrity or celebrities usually contribute a personal possession if they don't actually participate in the action.

Certainly you have heard or read of celebrity items of modest intrinsic value that command huge prices from the star-struck or collectors of mementoes: Lana Turner's sweater, Michael Jackson's sequined glove, Elvis's pink Cadillac, and even the bullet-ridden death car of Bonnie and Clyde.

While this plays to the passion many have for some association with the famous, it also has proved time and again to be an effective money-raiser. Some celebrities gladly participate because of the favorable public exposure it practically guarantees, others because of sincere dedication to the cause the auction will benefit.

And nearly everyone must have some experience of television auctions, in which the objects or services are hawked on the screen and viewers call in their bids. This form of salesmanship is used regularly to raise funds for public television stations and less frequently for other worthy causes.

Finally there is a practice lingering from older times and usually found at county fairs or organized picnics: the auction of box lunches, or blind dates, or even kisses. These are both fun- and fundraisers in which the sale items are donated by VIPs and the high bidders are usually good-spirited contributors to some cause.

Such celebrity auctions have little in common with the commercial varieties to which this book is principally devoted. Most people do not participate in such auctions hunting for bargains, even though some no doubt hope to profit from reselling celebrity items. Yet, if you've ever found yourself bidding at or witnessing such an affair, you have experienced at least the procedural aspects of most commercial auctions, and this should stand you in good stead if and when you decide to go bargain-hunting.

Charity Auctions

Quite similar is the charity auction. Here is where you are invited to pay huge sums for value-less items as a means of donating to charity. The form of the auction may be the same as a junk, antique, celebrity, or any other auction; only the purpose is different. And, to boot, you may be asked to pay admission to get in as a means of defraying the costs involved.

You participate, not in the expectation of coming out a winner, but as a generous donor to an organization or cause dear to your heart. And your accountant may even decide that what you spend at such an event is tax-deductible.

Still, on occasion, you may stumble across a good deal. Some charity auctions benefit from gifts donated by businesses. For the business owners, that can be good community relations and a tax deduction as well. One man, who hadn't even planned on a vacation, found himself the winner of an all-expenses-paid Caribbean cruise for two for a mere $850. It was donated by a local travel agency. So his charitable donation was a boomerang; he and his wife turned out to be beneficiaries.

A nationally recognized artist donated one of her paintings to a public television fund-raiser. Its real market value was $4,000 to $5,000. The sale, in the middle of the night, brought only $350, to the chagrin and embarrassment of the artist. The buyer made a coup!

You hardly bid at or contribute to a charity auction in the expectation of gain. If you come away from it with nothing more than experience, that will, like a celebrity auction, provide know-how that will be useful to you at a commercial auction, besides giving you a warm, cozy feeling.

Watch Out for Pitfalls

If, by any chance, your organization is planning to hold a charity auction, do not permit those involved to take the task lightly. Staging such a sale requires close attention to many fundamentals that all have to come together on the selected date in perfect coordination.

People considerations come first. Which among you have the organizing and technical abilities to comprise the working staff? Who will provide the items or services to be auctioned? What is the customer base, and how do you reach it? A misstep in answering any of these questions can doom the entire undertaking before it gets off the ground.

You need to start planning early because it takes time to round up donors, establish a date that won't conflict with other events of interest to your potential attendees, and to make the physical arrangements. You may want to consider retaining a professional auctioneer to help assure you aren't missing any bases and to conduct the sale itself.

One of my experiences is a lesson in things that can be poorly planned, mismanaged, and ultimately disappointing to most of those concerned. If you get into the complexities of planning for a charity auction, you may find it instructive.

A university publicly announced an "Alumni Auction". Faculty members, the school itself, and others would donate the items for sale. The audience for this event was carefully targeted: former administrators, local community leaders, students and faculty and, where the real potential profit lay, the public.

The locale designated for the auction was a prestigious country club. The fee for admission for those wishing to have lunch was steep and, for this part of the event, advance reservations were required. For those with no reservations, the fee was more modest and they were to go unfed.

Response to the initial announcement was overwhelming to those in charge of the event; requests for tickets far exceeded anything they had anticipated. Instead of being overjoyed, they decided to limit attendance by barring the public – from which the maximum earnings could be expected. With so limited a list of subscribers, the entire plan was changed. It became a high-priced dinner-dance to which only local dignitaries were invited.

In the end, items were still auctioned, but the relatively low volume of customers guaranteed a smaller financial bonanza. That was not the only negative result. The high cost of the dinner-dance excluded virtually the entire faculty and student body, turning off men and women who otherwise would have been strong supporters. One of the original objectives had been to encourage public knowledge and support of the university. Inviting them in, and then inviting them out, hardly advanced that aim.

Thus was a charity auction turned into an exclusive social event for the locally prominent, the potential financial benefit curtailed, and the ill-will of groups essential to the well-being of the university engendered. Although the event may have succeeded in raising funds, it was a calamity in human relations.

If a group endowed with all the talents of a university is capable of mishandling a charity auction this badly, it can happen to any voluntary organization. But it will not happen to you – if you know the pitfalls and avoid them.

Chapter Ten

Specialty Auctions

A lawyer we know is hooked on genuine oriental rugs. There is little he doesn't know about them. He will do almost anything to find and buy specimens he considers to be the very finest. You won't rub elbows with him at the ordinary auction house, where Fred and I and most of our friends look for oriental rugs, among other things. He attends only those auctions that are confined to the sale of the objects of his singular love. When he has reason to believe something special may be offered, he will fly thousands of miles to attend an oriental rug auction. He has purchased $40,000 oriental rugs for as little as $5,000. This is no penny-ante hobby, but the same drive to beat the financial odds that revs our motors is a force for collectors.

He is not alone, either in his preoccupation with a particular class of merchandise or in his single-mindedness in pursuing it. Thousands like him comb newspapers and trade publications for notices of specialty auctions and, when possible, get themselves on mailing lists for the auction houses and individual auctioneers that specialize in their fields of interest. Like people hooked on collecting stamps or coins, many men and women are so devoted to collecting *something* that they will go to great lengths and spend huge sums to satisfy their deeply embedded hungers. Specialty auctions are their meat.

Do not get the idea that everything auctioned by specialty houses is for the rich although such auctions, by and large, have a cachet you won't find at most junk auctions. My husband surprised me with a birthday gift that I treasure, picked up at a specialty auction. It is a first edition of the five-volume set of "Life of George Washington" by the renowned author Washington Irving, published in the 1850s. The bindings are somewhat shabby, but the set is complete. He paid only $27.50 for an item now assessed at about $200. Its value will likely increase markedly with the passage of time. But the fact is that companies or individuals can afford to hold specialty auctions only when their limited choice of merchandise is in high demand and can command suitable prices. For most of us that means the ante is higher at specialty auctions and, in some cases, well out of sight.

When an auction does make the newspaper headlines or the evening news on television, it's usually in connection with a specialty sale or an auction by one of the houses dealing in objects so expensive that these auction places are specialties to themselves. The name Sotheby's ring a bell?

Most of the decade of the 1980s was a dizzying auction era for industrialists, investors, and rich collectors. News of auctions by big-name houses reported scores of millions paid for single paintings.

The average citizen must have considered this conspicuous consumption indeed.

But news of high prices paid at specialty auctions is hardly confined to boom times. In early 1991, someone paid $20,210 for one of the 100 swatch watches produced in 1989 by Mimmo Paladino, who sold them for $70 each. A shirt worn in 1950 by Brooklyn Dodger Jackie Robinson sold for $16,093. Someone forked over $770,000 for a 1860 weather vane of a horse and rider. And *The New York Times* reported in January 1991 the highest price ever paid for a single piece of furniture: A gilded and inlaid Italian cabinet built for an English duke in the early 18th Century. The sale price: $15.2 million.

The variety of specialties is as great and as flexible as the tastes of collectors. But you won't find auctions advertised with the word "specialty" except on the rarest of occasions. They'll be labeled to define the nature of the merchandise. Some houses are noted for the specialties they regularly deal in. The well-known Christie's, for example, specializes in rare, usually high-priced, antiques and *objects d'art*. You don't go there looking for costume jewelry or barbeque spits. But Christie's and a substantial number of other established houses hold auctions for specialty items within such categories with some regularity. You won't hear about them unless you watch for the ads or request that your name be added to their mailing lists.

Nearly every large city has one or more established auction houses that avoid stocking ordinary goods but instead seek out merchandise of substantial value. Such marketers are the ones most likely to hold specialty auctions. They have various ways of getting out the word to known collectors by advertising in specialized publications, blanket mail notification, and even telephone calls to repeat customers.

Moreover many of these well-known houses employ auctioneers who are themselves specialists in such things as antique autos and machinery, jewelry, valuable paintings and sculptures, antique furniture, heraldry, etc. These specialists often are sent to distant locations to manage specialty auctions either because the goods are located out-of-town or as an accommodation to prospective customers.

A fair number of freelance auctioneers travel the nation to hold specialty auctions. If you are a collector, or even if you have an interest in one of the fields they represent, it can be worthwhile to learn who these specialists are and get yourself on the lists of potential customers to be informed in advance when a sale is to be held in or near your locality. If you are deep into a hobby, subscribe to a newsletter covering the field. In time you'll discover by reading in it who's who in the auction business of interest to you, and perhaps even the times and places of auctions you may want to attend.

Because the range of specialties stretches from baseball cards, to Elvis memorabilia, to jewelry, to violins, to zoo animals, I make no attempt to list all the applicable publications or membership organizations available to you. If you are a true collector, you are already up on such matters. If not, find others with similar interests and ask them to steer you.

Even for those collectors whose enthusiasm is less than red-hot, there is reason to attend a specialty auction or two, even if you've no intention to buy. Fred and I have attended several kinds of specialty auctions, sometimes planning to bid and other times just seeking information. We go when we want to see a particular auctioneer in action either because he's new to us or we've heard something interesting about his manner or methods. Attending specialty rug auctions, we have listened to and learned to converse in "rug language". While we're not experts, our knowledge gained in this way has enabled us to snag extremely good rug buys in other types of auctions.

Keep in mind that some auctions will no doubt be too rich for your blood – or for your pocketbook. But you don't have to be rich to attend.

Chapter Eleven

Government/Real Estate Auctions

The collapse of savings and loan institutions brought a whole new dimension to the governmental auction scene. The Resolution Trust Corporation was formed to dispose of the hundreds of billions in assets taken over by the federal government. These assets are comprised of nearly everything the mind can conjure up: factories and their contents, apartment, commercial and office buildings, co-ops and condominiums, houses, vacant land, vehicles and machinery of every variety, even non-paying loans made to individuals and corporations. A major task of the RTC was – and continues to be – turning all these assets into cash to help repay the vast outlays from the government.

Much of this is being disposed of through mammoth sales, many of them by auction, in volumes too great for the pocketbooks of most individuals. Corporations, other institutions, and monied investors are the principal buyers. Many of them turn around and sell some or all of these acquired assets through public auctions. And that's where you may come in. Real estate dealers and other business people, acting as agents for RTC, or as investors themselves, resell the properties one by one and often to the highest bidders at auctions. Also showing up at auctions are a broad scale of miscellaneous items acquired from the RTC as part of larger properties, such as furniture, office machinery, computers, etc. In effect, the U.S. Government is the primary source of billions in miscellaneous property turning up at auctions everywhere through the RTC alone.

While the Resolution Trust Corporation is the El Dorado of this trend, it is not by any means the only federal agency that disposes of property by auction. In 1991, for example, the General Services Administration sold some $100 million in government property, most of it through auctions or sealed bids. That makes it one of the world's great shopping malls, and the diversity of products offered runs from books to heavy machinery. You can get your name placed on the mailing list for catalogs by contacting the GSA regional office nearest you.

Disposing of surplus government property is one of the functions of this agency, so its offerings can be expected to continue indefinitely, while the RTC is trying to work itself out of a job. Indeed, it may do so in the next couple of years. Meanwhile, there is a whole world of other governmental sources for nearly any type of merchandise you can possibly desire. Refer to Appendix for information sources.

In his 494-page book *The Official Government Auction Guide*, George Chelekis lists more than a dozen federal entities that hold auctions and sets forth a compendium of information about each, including addresses and phone numbers as references for potential buyers. We know of no other reference work so all-encompassing in scope. It also includes information about state, county and city auctions. If your interest is high enough, we recommend acquiring this book. (Crown Publishers, Inc., New York, $25.)

Buying Land Blind

Our first purchase of government property was a piece of vacant land owned by the Veterans Administration. Reviewing a catalog that agency had supplied at our request, we found a 12-acre property in an area we "sort of" knew. This was a mail auction. We posted a bid and a cashier's check as a deposit, as required. Several weeks later we were notified that our bid was successful. We were elated. It was a steal.

We had scrutinized the map and parcel identification in the catalog. We knew our new property would let us walk to the shore of the man-made lake nearby, close to a resort town. All we had to do was cross a paved street, cast our lines into the water known to be great for fishing, and we had it made. We could hardly wait to see our new estate.

Some weeks later we drove the 500 miles to view our land. We found it. Indeed, as the map showed, it bordered on a paved road. As we began the drive we were delighted to discover the property was on the highest mountain peak in the area. Passing the last building before we turned onto the road that led to our property, we began to feel some concern. It had many signs warning "Low Water Crossing". There were narrow lanes over canyons in those places. We were still enthused about the beauty of the mountainside. We spoke of the splendor of our isolation, and, above all, of how wonderful it would be to have a place to fish with no interference by other anglers. We sought our boundary stakes and found them. The property was truly beautiful with the splendor of high mountain desert land. Out-croppings of rocks were flanked by prickly-pear cactus, occasionally interspersed by towering 100-year cactus in flower. The charm of the tree-lined canyons was intensified by our isolation; the nearest neighbor was five miles away.

But where was the lake? "Just across the road," said the map. We rushed the few feet to the yet unseen lake shore. Indeed, we could fish. We could fish, assuming we could cast down and reel up the 500-foot drop at the pathway's end. In astonishment, we stood atop the canyon wall and listened to the hum of power boats on the water below. Fishing from our "shore" was out of the question.

In months to come, still awed by the beauty of our place, we took steps to make it habitable. We put in a driveway on which to park the mobile home purchased for the purpose. I cleared a path to a large rock on the edge of the canyon. I dreamed of picking the prickly pears, canning them, and giving them away to friends. We spent nights in our trailer. We even spent a Thanksgiving on our mountaintop, occasionally driving the seven miles to the closest fishing spot. One day it rained. Water whipped to fury made our "low water crossings" impassable. Our enchantment vanished abruptly.

Not all such purchases are as disastrous. A close friend took a similar chance, but he was after property to hunt on. He purchased "blind" as we had, but with a different result. His property is perfect for his needs. He invites friends to hunt with him, and he thinks of his auction-property as a steal.

Still we have decided never to make such an investment without thoroughly knowing the place, the environmental conditions, and every other aspect of the property. If possible, we'd want to see it before buying. You may want to assure yourself in this way, too, if you consider acquiring real property at auction.

Local Government Auctions

On a smaller scale, state, county and local units of government acquire real property and other assets through tax forfeitures, seizures, bankruptcies, court orders, etc. And, like federal departments, they usually dispose of cars and other government-owned equipment from time to time. Sealed bid or open auctions are routinely advertised in classified sections of newspapers. In some jurisdictions, auctions are held periodically at predetermined times and places. Practices vary widely, so you will want to ascertain from the state treasurer's office, county sheriff's department, or city police chief's office what the practice is at your location. Many of these will also give you notification of upcoming sales by mail if you request that.

Most such auctions draw dealers or their agents as roses draw honeybees. While there may be many a thorn among the beauties offered, the thoughtful auctiongoer can expect to find excellent bargains in such things as office equipment, luxury items bagged in drug raids, and even automobiles. Police cars may be too beat up for your taste, but remember nearly every government office also uses vehicles.

Real Estate Auctions

Many real estate firms also sponsor home or business property auctions. This was once a rarity, but with the recession of the late 1980s and early 1990s and the consequent drop in property values, the practice has become more prevalent. Offering real estate for auction, rather than through negotiation, is a risk many owners approach reluctantly. Their only safeguard is to set a minimum price at which their homes or other properties may be offered at a private auction. Even that usually represents a woeful loss. The properties are consigned to a real estate auctioneer or firm. The auctioneer may demand a flat fee for conducting the auction, or may agree to a commission based on the sale amount. Often contents of the real property are offered in conjunction with the sale.

You may remember reading about the auction of some notable properties like the Mustang Ranch, the largest of Nevada's legal brothels. The building and its 330 acres went for $1.49 million. Everything was sold, down to a license plate imprinted "PIMP", bringing about $2 million from 1,200 bidders. The IRS had seized the property because of unpaid back taxes, penalties and interest.

Don't expect to find such a bonanza very often. More likely at any estate sale you'll find yourself brushing elbows with d evelopers, real estate agents, brokers, and other business people. They are expecting to resell or renovate property. People in such pursuits are sometimes directly notified of forthcoming offerings by the selling agents, and of course they study catalog listings.

Examining the Property

Several years ago, we saw a classified ad for such an auction of the property of a long-abandoned wholesale bakery-goods manufacturer. The auction site was a block-wide plant with adjacent yards. We reviewed the contents of the catalog received at registration and toured the building, although we had no interest in the the structure as a purchase. We saw huge commercial ovens, mixers, flour bins, refrigerators, and other items necessary to produce baked goods by the tens of thousands. We found lots of muffin, cake, pie, and bread pans, each lot containing 50 or more pans. Things we had never seen before were scattered among motors, coolers, and shelving.

By day's end, the building itself and everything in it had been sold. Some attendees purchased items for personal or business use, others for resale, and still others hauled away thousands of pounds of machinery to be sold as scrap metal. We took home a collage of bakery tools, proud owners of more than 100 bread, muffin, and pie tins. We paid $15. Our children and friends no longer want for such equipment.

The catalog listed "oven bricks" in a single lot almost buried in a distant corner of the bakery's yard. Waiting patiently until the lot came up, late in the day, we hoped no one else had it in their bidding sights. One lone individual offered $7.50 against our opening bid of $5. We won the "pad" – about 500 bricks – with our $10 counter bid. Today, our auction brick patio leads to brick paths surrounding a large pecan tree. We added two more pads of bricks to our original purchase, bought at retail, bringing the entire cost of our patio to under $300.

The Resolution Trust Corporation announced in November 1991 that its practice of auctioning off expensive properties by the lot was a success. In a nationwide offering, it sold thirteen out of fourteen commercial properties for $105 million. Success or not, it represented a loss to taxpayers and a bonanza to the purchasers, a dubious exchange if you are in a high tax bracket.

We decided to look into one such offering. We picked up a catalog and previewed the properties to be offered in the following week. The properties ran the gamut from small, odd-shaped lots to a 10-story office building. In such a milieu, we are small-timers indeed, but we could have made an offer on any of these properties, simply by following the detailed directions in the catalog. Some were within our price range but we decided to give this one a pass.

We later attended another RTC auction, this one of office equipment, to find out how it would be conducted. We joined more than 200 attendees and bought the catalog, sold for $5 by the firm contracted by RTC to handle the event. The property was nowhere in evidence. Yet the auctioneer took bids in rapid sequence on such diverse items as file cabinets, desks, refrigerators, paintings, and even plants. It was an audiovisual sale, a new procedure to us. As each item was flashed on the screen, bidders held up their bid cards and sales were made. Those present seemed to feel the auction was a winner.

Distressed properties at the turn of the decade of the 1990s brought huge private auction sales to the attention of the public. Citing the success of the RTC in combining properties and offering them at auction, for example, four large companies put together a package of properties valued at $500 million. They were Prudential Insurance Co. of America, Equitable Life Assurance Society, Trammell Crow Co., and Aldrich, Eastman & Waltch. In another private offering, owner Kirk Kerkorian decided to auction the Desert Inn and Casino at Las Vegas for about $200 million.

Calumet Farms, the famed breeding stable that produced Citation and Whirlaway among other celebrated bluebloods, went under the hammer in 1992. *The Wall Street Journal* reported the sale "included the farm's land and 17-room family residence, as well as its name and a cache of paintings, racing trophies, antique furniture, and other memorabilia".

MacGregor Sports went bankrupt and put up $2.2 million in equipment for auction. Clark Equipment put its forklift truck business on the block in 1991. Pacific Enterprises, a huge utility that had spent $2 billion to diversify into such things as drugstores, sporting goods stores, petroleum operations and even pecan groves, auctioned off some of its antique furniture and art when it ran into financial difficulties.

A troubled Homefed Bank was reported to have assembled a team of 500 persons to prepare bid packages on its $13.9 billion of assets. When a newly completed 26-floor condominium apartment building in Forest Hills, N.Y., ran into distress, it auctioned off 77 of the apartments that had originally been priced at $350 per square foot.

The total prices of the multitude of properties and collections of properties were dizzying. But as much of this merchandise reached the resale level, it became available to ordinary auctiongoers piece by piece and usually at bargain prices. The extent of this unprecedented movement of property to market is almost inconceivable to most individuals. The *Dow-Jones* financial wire, reporting on RTC operations in October 1991, said:

"By requiring buyers to take the bad with the good, the Resolution Trust Corp. is managing, despite the worst real estate market in decades, to sell some very poor properties, ranging from asbestos-tainted shopping centers to rat-infested apartments. The RTC has unloaded more than half the $344 billion in loans, securities and properties it has acquired. Moreover, it has recovered 95% of their $188 billion book value, taking in $179 billion in cash."

As this is written in early 1993, the RTC still has an inventory of billions, and predictions are that it will continue disposing of property for at least two years into the future, and possibly until 1996. While much of this will go directly to business and private investors, a staggering amount will ultimately find its way into retail auctions throughout the U.S.

With the economy slowly recovering early in 1993, including homebuilding and real estate sales, one has to wonder how long private auctions (contrasted with government auctions) of property will remain an ordinary part of the real estate scene. They were adopted in hard times, as a desperate measure by institutional and private owners to sell in an adverse market, usually at distress prices. For those interested in such bargains, scanning the legal notices and classified sections of newspapers can still reveal opportunities for you. In hundreds of localities, local real estate firms, as well as larger institutions, are still advertising good bargains on homes and business establishments acquired by the RTC or repossessed by lenders.

That means you probably won't find a better time than today or tomorrow to start studying the auction market for your dream home or vacation property.

Chapter Twelve

Dishonesty at Auctions

M any men and women fail to take advantage of auction sales because they suspect the field is characterized by fraud and misrepresentation. Word-of-mouth stories circulate among customers in this business – as they do in others – of crooked dealings: people buying what they think are antiques and finding later that they've overpaid for reproductions; fake paintings sold as genuine; the value of jewelry misrepresented; cars falling apart within days of purchase, etc. No doubt, in some cases, there is an element of truth here. In our own extensive experience, however, we have seen so little of this that we tend to discount most of it.

In all likelihood, such woeful tales stem from either the inexperience or the gullibility of the victims more often than the shenanigans of auction houses or auctioneers. But let's face it: some in the business are dishonest, although we believe they are few. So the newcomer to auctions should be prepared to reassure himself or herself by means we discuss here, and to recognize some of the telltale signs that suggest all is not on the up-and-up.

The owner of the business and the auctioneer (they are often different individuals although sometimes one and the same) control the quality of every commercial auction. Most owners are like businessmen everywhere: they strive to profit but realize that honest dealing is essential to survival. Their motivation is financial, moral, ethical. Anyone can establish an auction business, but few can long survive a reputation for dirty dealing.

Many auctioneers are far more footloose than owners who have established outlets. Some peddle their services as freelances, others cart their merchandise from place to place and hold auctions wherever they believe the market is. They have the opportunity, like impecunious circus owners, to set up their tents for a night or two and then slip off to find another audience. The opportunity to fleece customers is there. Few auctioneers take advantage of the opportunity because it means, if they are exposed, they can never return. But some persist in questionable practices. It would be reassuring if all auctioneers were licensed and thus subject to governmental oversight on a regular basis. In fact, only about half the states require licensing and put other restraints on auctioneers. Some counties or municipalities have their own requirements. But there is no uniform national system to reassure customers and potential customers.

Licensing

The 5,500 members of the Natonal Auctioneers Association, based in Overland Park, Kans., are governed by codes of standards and ethics, and most of them are proud to display the NAA emblem at business establishments. The NAA sponsors a continuing series of educational workshops and seminars to upgrade the qualifications of auctioneers, as do the state branches of the organization. Beyond this, some auctioneers use the initials CAI (for Certified Auctioneers Institute) after their names. These are NAA members who, after two years as full-time auctioneers, have successfully passed a three-year program in auction business management at Indiana University. While neither the NAA emblem nor the CAI honor guarantees the integrity of its user, it's about as close as a novice auction attendee can come to assuring himself or herself of dealing with honest business people.

The basis for issuing licenses varies among the thirty-two states that mandate them. Most require that the auctioneer-applicant must have legitimate experience extending over a specified period of time, must show evidence of schooling in the specialty, and must demonstrate knowledge of state regulations governing auctions. Such regulations set forth the rules of conduct for auctions and provide legal remedies for customers who can show the auctioneer's failure to comply. Infractions by an auctioneer can result in the license withdrawal.

In the states with such legislation, consumers have clearly mandated recourse to the law. They may bring civil suits – and in some cases criminal suits – against the auctioneer or auction houses to recover losses. State-sanctioned auctioneers customarily provide their license numbers on business cards and in advertising and in some jurisdictions are required to do so. If an aggrieved customer questions the legitimacy of the auctioneer's credentials, an investigation can be stimulated by complaining to the office of the secretary of state, which will assign that function to the appropriate state agency.

Licensed auctioneers can, in many states, have apprentices. The apprentice can conduct an auction temporarily using the licensed auctioneer's number. After an apprentice has conducted six such apprenticeship auctions in a year's time, in some states they can apply to take the state's auctioneer license examination. In some states, an individual owner of a home and/or contents can auction his or her own property once a year, without a license. Because of these different legal circumstances, your best bet, if you have a question or a problem, is to contact the office of the secretary of state in which you are a current resident.

Most men and women who plan careers as auctioneers attend auction schools, which operate throughout the country, although the majority are in midwestern states. The purpose is not so much to learn the rules of auction conduct as to study techniques, including the development of the sing-song manner popular with some auctioneers, although by no means all of them. But knowing the rules and developing an "auctioneer's patter" does not necessarily make a good auctioneer or, for that matter, an honest one.

Bid Rigging

There is one form of dishonesty that can cheat not only the potential buyer but the auctioneer and the house as well. It is known as bid-rigging. In this dodge two or more conspirators – usually dealers or wholesalers – agree in advance on the price for an object (or a lot) to be auctioned and designate one of their members to do the bidding, while the others forgo their bids.

That takes the competition out of the auction and, when it is successful, guarantees the bidding ring a favorable price. Rings tend to show up at auctions marketing many like items, according to *The Auctioneer Magazine*.

"After the auction," the article explains, "the group meets with a list of what they bought. They then hold another auction among themselves, re-auctioning the newly acquired property. The difference between what the ring paid at the first auction and what a member of the group bids for it at the secondary auction is divided proportionally. There are many variations to this scenario..."

Auctioneers are trained to recognize and discourage bid-rigging, which is not only unethical but illegal, but they are sometimes unaware of it and at other times helpless to stop it. Bid-rigging is most likely to take place at poorly attended auctions and least likely to succeed when the non-dealer audience is large and the bidding lively.

The effect of this scam on buyers? "They may find the price of their prospective purchases driven sky high by ring members to discourage future bidding for fear of paying artificially inflated prices. These buyers may eventually stop attending auctions where these dealers are present."

Any honest auctiongoer who feels he's being victimized in this way should report it to a federal law enforcement agency. Price-fixing is a felony that carries heavy penalties for those found guilty.

Recognizing the Honest Auctioneer

Veteran auctiongoers disagree about the qualities that differentiate a good auctioneer from a bad one, but all do agree that a lack of integrity is always the mark of a poor one. If any auction you attend is presided over by an auctioneer who has stayed in business in the same locale for a reasonable period of time, or one who returns to your locale from time to time to hold intermittent auctions, he is probably straightforward and deserves your trust. That is because the auctioneer is always the key to success or failure of an auction house or individual sale. Professionals attend auctions with enough regularity to learn the players, much as baseball fans do. If you don't find the pros in attendance, there is probably a good reason, and that should be enough to get you up on your toes and observe closely what's going on.

Moreover, auction buffs circulate information about auctioneers by word of mouth, so that auctioneers with shaky reputations soon become known to regular attendees. The novice will probably not be in that conversational circuit but will have to rely on experience and intuition to spot a phony – unless you begin your auction adventures with an experienced friend in tow. How this works can be illustrated with an experience we've had.

An auctioneer-owned house opened for business with some advertising fanfare, which is unusual in this business. He had no competition for the Friday night time slot, so the buffs in the town were eager to test his wares. Fred and I were laggards and didn't get to the new shop for several weeks. By then, linked into the word-of-mouth network, we knew the man was dishonest and used questionable techniques. As happens with the borderline operators, he soon packed up his goods for lack of customers and, presumably, opened up elsewhere in an endless round of vexatious moves brought on by his own thickheadedness.

Good auctioneers have certain abilities in common, including those associated with professional salespersons, and a touch of the psychologist's skills, and even those of an entertainer. The good auctioneer imperceptibly controls the audience, using the skills of the trade and his sense of the customers' needs. Veteran attendees can almost "smell" a good auctioneer, regardless of his or her techniques or style, just as they can detect a dishonest one no matter how good the auctioneer may superficially appear.

Reliable auctioneers develop a clientele. Regulars follow the auctioneers they trust, sometimes because of the merchandise offered; sometimes because of the auctioneer's efficient management of the proceedings; and sometimes because of the auctioneer's style. Auction houses rely on a solid, stable clientele that will appear at their auctions over and over again, and for this reason try to find and hold onto good auctioneers. The clientele is dominated by dealers, collectors, or investors. Nearly every auction also draws novices, but not in sufficient numbers to justify the cost of holding an auction for them alone.

The good auctioneer knows this and doesn't take the risk of running off his regulars by trying to take advantage of the newcomers. A novice auction-eer with larcenous intent sometimes overestimates his ability to hoodwink the audience and still remain in business. Even experienced auctioneers scanty on ethics can fall into this trap, like the man who began his business on Friday nights. Within two weeks, word had spread that he regularly committed an unforgivable auction sin: he "bid against the wall". By the time we finally went to his auction, we were aware of his practice. It had been tested in the first week. We had also heard that he had some excellent general merchandise to offer. So we attended, pre-pared to try to outwit him. Unfortunately, we did not find anything we wanted. By the time we were ready to test him again, he had fled to a new town.

Bidding against the Wall

What is "bidding against the wall"? Simply, it is the auctioneer raising the bid price by pretend-ing there is a challenging bid somewhere in the room, out of sight of the real bidder or bidders. When this gimmick succeeds the house profits, but the winning bidder pays an artificially inflated price. On an individual sale, it hardly seems worth the effort. If the auctioneer can put together some moderate and high-priced sales, he substantially increases his commission or the house profit.

Stacking the House

Another dishonest technique is stacking the house. We recently attended such a stacked-house auction, as did some other regulars, and a fair number of novices. It soon became apparent to the regulars that three women novices were either very poor judges of values, or they were shills for the auctioneer. This of course aroused our suspicions and that evening few of us purchased anything. Some unidentifiable attendees did make purchases, bidding against outrageous prices offered by the suspect women for very unimpressive items. The auctioneer appeared unfazed by these outlandish bids, and this was a telling clue to the regulars because most good auctioneers will raise an eyebrow when this happens.

Of course, auctioneers cater to those buying, and particularly to those buying frequently, or paying high prices for low-value merchandise. That's how they earn a living. But the best of them won't allow even novices to make fools of themselves in the presence of the regular clientele. As the evening progressed, other regulars entered the auction house. Finally, one recognized the women. They were friends of the auctioneer's wife. They were shills.

The function of a shill in any business is to increase the house take by luring paying customers to spend more than they had intended. This may be a legitimate operation for a circus sideshow or in a gambling casino (though few losers would think so). In the auction businesss, shills are not acceptable. Their presence – when customers can identify them – marks the auctioneer as dishonest or at best unethical. Novices may not recognize the signs of a shill in the audience but, if a regular spots the shill, he or she will likely tip off others in attendance. Buffs share a camaraderie, and this is evidence of it. Still, it is best to keep your eyes open.

The "Leave a Bid" Option

Most auction houses offer a service to their clientele, both regulars and novices. The service is the "leave a bid" option. If, for instance, an individual previews merchandise, but cannot stay or return for the actual bidding, the auctioneer will take a sealed bid. The bid is actually the non-attending individual's offer of a maximum price he or she will pay for a specified item. When bidding on the item opens, the house, often the auctioneer's clerk, will bid on behalf of the absent individual. This is a truly helpful service, when the auctioneer or house is honest. Often maximum bids may never be reached in the open bidding, and the sealed bid may win the bid at a price lower than the maximum offered. On the other hand, some less than honest auctioneers, or auction management, may pretend there is a sealed bid, when there is not. Or they may unwarrantedly raise the bid to the maximum the non-attendee was willing to pay. Either method is unethical because it takes unfair advantage of trusting customers while they are absent.

On one occasion this happened to us. We left a sealed bid for a sofa while we went off on another errand. The auction house clerk called us to tell us we had won. Later, friends notified us that our sofa had a nearest bid $15 less than the jump to our maximum of $50. Our response? We never again left a sealed bid with that house, although we still attend the auction because it has good merchandise and a skillful auctioneer. However, we are now skeptical of the ethics. The best advice to newcomers to auctions remains: "Buyer beware".

The Owner's role

Let me clarify the use here of the terms "auctioneer" and "house-owner or -manager". Many auctioneers own their own auction houses. Other houses are owned by non-auctioneers who hire freelances to come in and conduct the auctions. The standard method is to pay freelances a flat fee in addition to a small percentage of the total take of an auction. What difference does the ownership make to the attendees? In most instances, none.

Yet sometimes you will see the auctioneer turn to the house-owner to ask about a particular item, or about what kind of auction sale will be used on various items. He may ask the owner's permission to accept a single bid as a final purchase on an item. The difference between the auctioneer-owned and other houses is the role of the owner. When the owner is in evidence at an auction, and is in frequent contact with the auctioneer, be alert to what they are talking about. It may have an impact on your bidding decisions.

The auctioneer may even have the house-owner at his side, although this can be distracting for the audience We still laugh about our experience at an out-of-state auction. The auctioneer's technique was excellent, as was the merchandise. But he would no sooner identify a piece of merchandise and start the bidding, when the owner interrupted to elaborate on something, or to set forth other information for the bidders. This occurred throughout the auction. We were embarrassed for the auctioneer and hoping his fee had been set high. And we were exhausted trying to keep up with the continuous interruptions. There is no need for buyers to stand for such nonsense. We suspect the auctioneer later forced the owner to clarify their roles, or refused to work for him again, or, most likely, the auction business failed.

Chapter Thirteen

Auctioneers:
Love/Hate Relationships

It would be hard to overstress the importance of the auctioneer. We're going to refer to that individual here as "he" because very few women are auctioneers at present. But hold your hats: more women are attending auction schools; women are achieving more success and prominence, and the breed is growing fast, as you'll see in the section of this chapter dealing with women auctioneers.

The auctioneer not only controls the proceedings, but his personality, his knowledge of the merchandise, his degree of empathy with the audience, his style, and his pace all set the tone that makes attending an auction a chore or a memorable occasion. People who really care about auctions and spend part of their lives attending them develop a taste for auctioneers, as wine-lovers develop a taste for and a critical discernment about different wines and vintages.

In time, the auction buff often finds himself or herself deciding whether to attend an auction as much by what is known or thought about the auctioneer as about the merchandise to be offered. The scale of auctioneers ranges from the bad and indifferent to the magnetic. This is of minor consequence to the novice, of course, because the primary lure of an auction is the expectation of paying low for something high in value. Even for the newcomer to auctions, though, it is reassuring to know that you need not be discouraged, even if you run up against an auctioneer or two who arouse about as much enthusiasm as a cold rain; there is always another auction. It also helps if you can peg an auctioneer into a category that suggests how you can best react with him.

There is a category of auctiongoers – I consider them cynics – whose distrust of auctioneers is total. They will tell you that the auctioneer's business is to sell, sell, sell at the highest possible price by whatever means he can devise.

"The art of auctioneering," one man said, "is ten-tenths persuasion. He'll induce the reluctant to bid by sweet talk, intimidation, and truth-twisting. He is never satisfied with a bid and will do anything in his bag of tricks to sell, humor or shame bidders ever higher. He works on commission and all the training he undergoes, all the practicing he does, and all the efforts he makes while holding the gavel are for no other purpose than to push up his income. I wouldn't trust one as far as I could shove him with my pinky."

That's another way of saying "buyer beware". Fred and I have met such auctioneers rarely, although they certainly exist. Unless you bring an extreme wariness to all your decisions, there is no point in being this cynical; it can spoil your fun and probably won't knock a nickel off a winning bid.

The Colonels

The "colonels" are always past middle age and sometimes deep into senior citizenship. Their demeanor of authority is inescapable. If they also have good auction techniques, they become the favorites of regular attendants. And they're not confined to any given area. You'll find them scattered throughout the auctioneer's world. We have seen colonels working at junk, antique and fine jewelry auctions.

The popularity of this breed is such that some businesses advertise themselves as "Colonel Blank's Auction House", using the man's first or last name. If that conjures up for you the vision of a Civil War officer dressed in blue or gray, sword at side and hat squarely aboard his head, maybe that's the intent. He's a father-figure, likeable, gently domineering: "You, you, would dare question me, the colonel?"

The prevalence of colonels in the business is manifest in many ways. The Missouri Auction School in Kansas City sells a public-address system known as Colonel 500. Colonel W. Craig Lawing of Charlotte, N.C., advertises three versions of an "auctioneer" hat. The Worldwide College of Auctioneering in Mason City, Iowa, is owned by Col. Gordon E. Taylor.

No one does question the validity of the colonel's title. He's old enough to have served in wartime. There are any number of localities and organizations that freely bestow this honorary title. It's even possible to buy a title, though no one who does is likely to admit it. The legitimacy or lack thereof doesn't really matter, for the title is merely the tag for a certain kind of personality, a personality that many readily recognize and accept. And it gives the auctioneer the aura of authority that he surely believes – even if no one else does – lends his pitch a certain panache.

And he's not to be made fun of. Bidders always address him as "Colonel" or risk a public rebuke. I myself will get his attention by calling out "Colonel?" and feel no uneasiness about it. And the auction-house personnel – the ringmen, clerks and even owners – also fall into line. You, as a tyro at auction-shopping, could do worse then get your auction baptism under the colonel's cool eye. He wants to be known as firm but impartial. He's not likely to let a newcomer be chivvied about. That is, assuming he's honest.

The Cowboys

This is a younger crowd with certain stylistic demands. For many cowboys, the image is a matter of dress, which may dictate the manner of conducting an auction. Cowboy auctioneers are "down home". They wear cowboy hats. The cowboy will push up the brim when he questions a low price bid. He will loop his fingers into the ever-present belt – with appropriate buckle – as he puzzles over an item's description. At some point of feigned disgust with an audience, he will roll up his sleeves, very slowly, the way a real cowboy might roll a cigarette, as a means of finding space to think.

The cowboy leans toward his audience, seeming to puzzle over their actions. Whereas the colonel slouches in the comfort of his superiority or stands in command of his troops, the cowboy rides astride his audience. Rather than a podium or floor used by most auctioneers, the cowboys prefer to auction from ladders.

For most of these auctioneers, the cowboy routine is a finely-honed act, a rehearsed role, an assumed identity, adopted for a single reason: it often works. In time the cowboy act becomes second nature and is therefore believable. They often conduct excellent auctions and are therefore generally popular with auction regulars. But I can't say often enough: keep your eyes and options open.

The Chanters

If you've never attended an auction, the chanter is the auctioneer you expect to see, but probably won't. Through conscious effort exerted over years of manipulating the gavel, chanters have developed rapid-fire speech patterns. Country-singer fans may be familiar with Hank Snow. His decade-old hit record "The Auctioneer" is an excellent imitation of the chanter.

And although this is the presentation many novices expect to find on their first excursion to an auction house, chanters are mostly specialists. They call for bids in their peculiar lingo mainly at auctions of commodities like tobacco, corn, coal and the like; livestock, and other items of interest primarily to professional buyers. They are rarely found at an auction likely to attract casual retail buyers. No doubt that's a good thing because chanters are difficult to understand and could prove intimidating to the novice.

Describing the auctioneer's chant is like trying to explain yodeling. The chant is a string of indistinguishable words, interspersed with verbal notations of offers. Experts in attendance have no problem with this. They too are professionals, and they respond with winks, nods, scratches and hand-flicks, among other signs readily interpreted by the auctioneer. Often these signs are deliberately baffling because bidders do not want the competition to know their offers.

Tyros bring another cliche to their first auctions: the image of the auctioneer crying, "Going, going, gone!" I know of novices who waited for this call as signalling the end of a bid sequence. By the time they realized it did not occur, the auctioneer had moved onto another lot for bid. The chanters – and most other auctioneers – simply cry "Sold" when a high bid is reached, and then continue to the next lot.

Does all this mean the newcomer should avoid chanter auctions? Not at all. The key to bidding in such auctions is not wholly in understanding the auctioneer's every word, but in recognizing when a bid has been made and jumping in with a bid between chanter sounds. Chanters run fast auctions – as many as 60 to 90 items per hour – and don't usually engage in banter with the audience. Because of the rapidity and intensity of the proceedings, few regulars will offer to help novices and may even be annoyed at questions from outsiders. Yet, if the thought of this kind of auction appeals to you, and there's something you want to buy at one, go ahead and try your hand. But don't put in a bid until you're sure you understand what's going on.

The Freelances

Freelance auctioneers come in all flavors; dress, approach and styles are optional. They are as various in personality and temperament as the audiences they serve. They share little in common but their trade, and each has his own approach to the business. Most make an effort to present an attractive personality. Some are take-me-or-leave-me types, all business. Some are even colonels or cowboys.

Occasionally you'll run across one who is sarcastic, or impatient, or haughty, or arrogant. In such cases, keep in mind that you're not there to attend a show; you are looking for a bargain. Nevertheless, the freelance auctioneer, assuming he can build a following, is a potent addition to the lure of the auction.

What makes him distinctive is that he is an (often temporary) employee rather than an owner. Any decision that he makes before starting the bidding on a lot can be overruled. He is in charge of the bidding process only, and you may expect to see him interrupt the proceedings from time to time to square away a question or problem with the owner or manager of the house. That means you can hardly criticize the auctioneer for the items put to bid, the minimum prices that may be specified, or any other aspect of the auction process. Where the owner and auctioneer are in good sync, usually after they've worked together for a while, everything goes smoothly and problems rarely arise.

Auctioneering is hard work, so on a big sale, or one that may last all day, two or more auctioneers may share the load. One of our favorite auctions, held monthly, was a day-long affair, conducted by the owner and a freelance auctioneer. The two men rotated the job about every hour. One had a "patter" style and was very fast. The owner was slow-paced. Their styles contrasted sharply. For the regulars, the change of pace made the long day more interesting than it might otherwise have been, but it tended to frustrate novices.

Complaints to the freelance auctioneer or the owner about the other's style became a contentious element of the sale. Ultimately the freelance complained privately to us and others that he was always stuck with calling the ends of the auctions because of his speed. This led in time to a split between them. The owner now does the auctioneering with an occasional apprentice taking over during the breaks, while the freelance works other auctions throughout the metropolitan area and remains a favorite with frequent auctiongoers.

I've written here much about style, which is almost impossible to describe with precision, but let me make a stab at it.

Catalogs are not available at every auction, although they are an important means of simplifying the work for everyone and are therefore commonly used. The catalog may be as fancy as a full-color brochure or as simple as a mimeographed, numbered list of items to be auctioned, with a brief description of each lot. It is the catalog from which bidders and auction-house personnel alike work. When there is no catalog, the auctioneer describes the lot orally before starting the bidding.

The auctioneer's style first shows in the manner in which he introduces an item. Some simply call out the lot number and the bidding starts: "Lot 137". Others might call: "Lot 137, Books", just as listed in the catalog. If there is no catalog, the books may be held up by the "ringman" for the audience. Another auctioneer might call out: "Lot 137, some really fine books," and then point out some of them. Still another may enthuse over the books, even passing one or two around for the audience to inspect.

The time taken, the manner of presenting the item, the degree of salesmanship involved, and the personality of the auctioneer give an indication from the outset of his style. It is a tipoff as to what to expect of him throughout the auction. Obviously, all of us being individualists, we are charmed by some auctioneers, turned off by others, or indifferent as we pursue our own ends unaffected by the intermediary. Yet, for those who spend any amount of time at auctions, an unappealing style tends to spoil the fun.

Fortunately, that spoliation is likely to be temporary because of the nature of freelancing. Unsuccessful freelances don't get to remain long in one place. If they prove unpopular, if they fail to meet financial goals consistently, if they can't get along with the house-owner or -manager, if they engage in questionable practices — then the "free" in their titles is what they in fact become.

The Patterers

Auctioneers who use a patter come close to what the inexperienced attendee expects from the radio and television auction commercials he or she has heard. It is extremely fast talk, sometimes coming through more as a hum than speech except for requests for bids and the call of bids made. Interestingly, much of this spouting by some auctioneers is meaningless, consisting of sounds developed to attain a level of enthusiasm on the part of the audience. Other patterers are actually saying something in a rapid sing-song, usually describing or praising the item, or urging you to bid. Newcomers may be utterly in the dark when this happens. But don't worry. What's important is the bidding process, and most auctioneers of every stripe make sure you hear that loud and clear.

What the patterer does demand of you is close concentration and tolerance for doing business in the fast lane. Attendance at this kind of auction does not allow much time for discussion with friends or fellow attendees. It does assure you that no time is wasted; the auction will cover the agenda in a hurry.

The auctioneer's patter comes close to the specialist's chant. Indeed you'll experience it most frequently at antique, auto and estate auctions. And, although it's not as mysterious as the chant, auctioneers have to work hard to develop it at school and/or in practice sessions.

A father and son auctioneer team we know has been holding a weekly sale at the business they own for more than 30 years. Their patter is so similar that we are confident the younger learned it by studying his old man. The efficiency of this team is not hampered because of the almost unintelligible patter they use between the clear-cut announcements of bid offers and wins.

They both sound something like this: "Do I hear a $50 on the desk?" No response from the audience. "$25?" A bid is made. The auctioneer:

"$25, aaaa, zzzz, qqqq, tttt, $25, zzzz" Another bid appears and "$27.50, aaa, and I have $30, $32.50, bbbb, ssss, ttttt, rrrr, $35! Last call! This is a fine desk. $35, aaaa, bbbb, zzzz, once, twice, sold!" This is all done very rapidly, and the auctoneer immediately moves on to sell the next item or lot.

Regulars know when to listen and act, taking little time for considering the value or meaning of the sounds the patter auctioneer makes. The only explanation any auctioneer has been able to give me is that his voice keeps the attention and excitement of the audience up. Of course, stimulating auction fever is an aim of every auctioneer, and surely they have evidence that the use of such patter helps do that. And I guess it's better than "$25?" Silence, silence, silence. "$27.50" Silence, silence, and so on.

The Social Directors

Conducting a hard-nosed business event in a social setting is an art a substantial number of owner/auctioneers have developed to build repeat business. It's good for the entrepreneur. For many of us who are auction buffs, this also makes attending more of a pleasure and fosters acquaintanceships that can develop into friendships. Whether this kind of atmosphere appeals to you is a matter of taste. If you are reasonably gregarious and enjoy buying in a relaxed setting without losing the value of purchasing at auction, seek out one run by a social director type.

The techniques auctioneers devise to hype the business are extremely diverse and not always designed to tickle the customer's fancy. The social director style of auctioneering is the reverse. It's a subtle pitch for your loyalty and repeat business; it caters to your comfort and your ego, tries to make a friend of you, imposing the obligations that go with friendship.

Don't confuse this with the open hand or the spirit of philanthropy. It is the sugar some auctioneers add to a deal with the expectation of attracting more flies. In the end, whatever the auctioneer's purpose, you are there to discover a steal, and you can do that in either a warehouse or a living-room environment. When the business gets under way, the auctioneer and his customer are adversaries and neither should let friendship fog up the air.

Let me describe an auction, presented by a social director auctioneer, that Fred and I sometimes attend. His place of business is a large, comfortable, well-lit building. Instead of walking you around the furniture items for sale, he arranges the chairs, sofas and other furniture into conversational groupings for use by potential bidders during the auction. Food is often available, either free or at modest cost, and he sometimes adds a grace note by serving wine and cheese – at no charge. The pace of the auction is slow, in keeping with the conversational aura he has created.

After you've been there two or three times, he addresses you by name and will provoke conversation by asking an innocent question: "How's your family?" You bid here with hand-held numbered cards, but he'll address the winning bidder by his or her first name, at the same time offering thanks. He may even praise a non-winner for making it an interesting auction.

All of this does have its effect. When he says something like "Aw, come on, guys," if he's having trouble getting an auction started or reaching a reasonable price, some are inclined to make a low bid or jump into the bidding process just to help out. Such palsy-walsy doings turn some newcomers off and they walk out. More often they become regulars.

One auctioneer of this ilk changed his style one day when he had a particularly large consignment of auction items. He eliminated the social aspects of the affair to speed up the proceedings. This appalled the regulars in attendance. He later told me he received so many complaints that he returned to his accustomed social style and never again put on the rush.

Are higher prices paid at this type of auction? On occasion, perhaps, when a regular jumps into the bidding to help the auctioneer. On the whole, it is my experience this doesn't happen very often and then represents hardly more than a token jump. This usually occurs when only one bid is made on an item, which means that it can't be sold. That one bid also indicates the merchandise has little, if any, attraction to most attendees. The second (friendly) bid usually assures a sale to the original bidder at slightly more than his or her opening offer. Certainly I wouldn't discourage a newcomer from attending a social director-style auction. Many will find it more simpatico than any other kind of auction sale.

The Sophisticates

Informality is the mode of most auctions. Some are positively grubby, requiring the attendees to deal with dusty stock and manhandle the merchandise to assess its value. Others are more orderly, and some are even spotless and have a recognizable organization, but are lacking in amenities. Few regulars bother to dress up for the occasion, and auction-house personnel reflect the informal tone and dress of their audiences. An exception may be the type of auction we have described as "social", at which regulars usually appear in dress appropriate for business or informal dining out.

But there is a kind of auction that falls short of the tony, salon style of high-priced houses like Sotheby's and Christie's, yet is several cuts above the common auction in formality. Such auctions may fall short of what you or I would consider stiff but are certainly more highly organized and far less casual than most auctions. Such sales are run by what Fred and I and other buffs consider "sophisticated auctioneers".

A single clue will tip you off – the seating arrangement. When all chairs are lined up theater-style in aisles with name-tags on the chairs for regulars, you can be pretty sure you're about to be exposed to an "auctioneer sophisticate". You probably won't see him before the proceedings begin because the sophisticate tends to hole up in his office, to which you have no access unless you have made expensive purchases on earlier occasions.

When the auction is about to begin, the sophisticate doesn't saunter to the podium; he makes an entrance. The sophisticate gives the impression that the business is really beneath his dignity; that is, he appears disdainful of any merchandise that isn't expensive and he sometimes tends to be overbearing with his potential customers. I have never seen a sophisticate auctioneer who didn't wear a three-piece suit, a dress shirt and tie. His clerk, usually an attractive young woman, is coiffed in the latest style and wears designer clothes. The auctioneer's watch is always expensive and if the clerk's jewelry isn't real you'll never know it without getting your teeth on the pearls.

Such a setting also calls for burnishing the merchandise. It's almost always in excellent condition, or at least as good as it can be made to appear. Furniture is polished. Spotlights may be placed to allow helpers to showcase the best features. The auctioneer introduces items by title but rarely gives any additional information. He assumes he has a sophisticated audience because this kind of auction invariably draws dealers, but he is also hoping to flatter the innocent by this ploy.

If dealers dominate the audience, the price the auction commands is not likely to exceed the value of the merchandise. But the novice may well be drawn into offering much higher bids than are justified, responding to this kind of manipulation. So be on your guard. Remember to discontinue the bidding when you've reached what you have decided in advance is the maximum any given item or lot is worth to you. The glitter, the haughtiness of the auctioneer, the obvious appeal to class-consciousness add up simply to another gimmick to increase the house take.

My husband and I often attend two auctions run by sophisticates. The auctioneers are good, despite the act, as is the merchandise. We've made occasional purchases. For example, we paid only $70 for a very old mahogany and teakwood oriental chest, purchased at the tail end of a sale after most others had left. It's a good idea to keep in mind that dealers leave as soon as the merchandise interesting them has been sold, and many regulars stay only long enough to bid on the one or two objects that have captured their fancy. Often, at the end of an auction, there aren't enough bidders to stage a heated competition, a great time for real bargains.

One auctioneer of this variety whom we know holds auctions on an erratic basis. He advertises them and mails out notices to regular attendees. This is not an uncommon procedure. This sophisticate auctioneer plays the dishonest "bidding-against-the-wall" routine but, since we know that, we scrutinize the bidding like a housewife looking for evidence of cockroaches. Our intent is to outwit him, and most of the regulars do.

Another sophisticate auctioneer has become a favorite with Fred and me. He and his wife have made their auction the current rage in an exclusive suburb, and the sessions are dominated by private individuals anxious to add to their expensive homes. Their proclivity for paying high prices has shooed most dealers away. By waiting out the majority of the audience, we have been able to purchase some excellent pieces, often English, at very good prices.

The show put on by sophisticate auctioneers makes your attendance worthwhile at least once. While the regulars may be playing games at such affairs, even the amateur can sometimes find good quality merchandise at surprisingly low prices. Another word of caution: Much of the atmospherics are staged to encourage auction fever. Inspect the merchandise in advance, decide what you want and the maximum you're willing to pay, and stick to your guns.

The Talkers

So what auctioneer isn't a talker? The colonels, cowboys, chanters, freelances, patterers and sophisticates gush language as voluminously as the taps in your bathtub spout water. Sing-song language comes as readily to auctioneers as milk to cows. What distinguishes the talker auctioneer is the lack of chant, patter, or sing-song. He just, well, talks. He's a conversationalist. No cryptic language from him. No matter how large the audience or how extensive the agenda, he carries on as if he's sitting in your living room, discussing the merchandise.

That makes for a slow-going auction and turns off a surprising number of potential buyers. The talkers are few because most of them find their relaxed style leads to few sales and, in time, digs the abyss of failure in the auction business. We haven't found these relaxed individuals very often, but when I cross one's threshold my entrance is usually the prelude to a quick retreat. Unlike me, Fred is a mound of malleable patience. He can wait, bored, for the bidding to move along, often winning his lot by sheer endurance.

The talker offers one advantage to patient buyers. The merchandise at his auctions is usually low in price but it takes three to five minutes to move each item. This sends eager potential buyers crowding out the doors. By the time they've gone, the dreamers with stamina who remain are few, and that

132

reduces competition and therefore the size of winning offers. Maybe Fred's discovered something good. But if you follow his lead, bring a good book or your knitting. It may be a long wait.

The Women

Nobody seems to know how many women are qualified auctioneers or owners of auction-houses. Informed estimates range from 8% to 10%, but there is general agreement in the industry that the volume is growing, though at perhaps a slower rate than in businesses that are less dominated by men.

Paul Dewees, who says his Missouri Auction School is the oldest and largest, finds that the fastest-growing facet of the auction business is the entry of women. He sponsored a recent national survey that discovered about 8% of auctioneers are women. "If we'd done the survey 15 years ago," he commented, "I figure the figure would have been close to zero or one percent."

When women first began training as auctioneers, their interest leaned toward antiques and horse auctions. Today there are no such ceilings; the sky's the limit. Kristy Ogle, owner of the newer Texas Auction Academy, says about ten percent of her students are women, and as graduate auctioneers they do very well. "It's just an opinion, but I believe that many women are able to get more money out of a crowd than a man could," she said.

Veterans agree there have always been women in the auction business. Most houses are family-owned. Wives, sisters, daughters have acted as clerks, cashiers and other functionaries from the beginning, but rarely as auctioneers. That seems to be changing rapidly now. The number of husband-and-wife auctioneer teams is growing. Moreover, said Mr. Dewees, once women graduates start building a clientele they're well on the way toward establishing their own businesses. Many who began their training five to seven years ago, he believes, "now have very good businesses."

Auctioneer schooling is not the only way women have successfully entered the business. *Forbes* magazine told the story of Leslie Hindman, who learned the business in Chicago as an assistant in the office of the world-renowned Sotheby's in 1978. Years later, she formed her own business as a struggling enterprise that has grown into one of the city's foremost auction-houses, competing with her earlier employer and realizing millions of dollars in annual sales.

And in March 1993, Sotheby's promoted Diana D. Brooks from her already impressive post as president and chief executive officer of North and South American auction operations to head the company's worldwide auction businesses. Sotheby's has 140 offices around the globe, some of which also participate in the firm's financial and real estate businesses.

With this appointment, Mrs. Brooks became perhaps the most powerful force in the world's auction markets. Not bad in a field that has traditionally been male-dominated.

Chapter Fourteen

What to Expect at Your First Auction

If you have never attended an auction, that first visit can be bewildering, particularly if you find yourself in a crowd. It helps to know in advance how an auction is organized and manned, what the procedures are, and how you can best carry out your role if you decide to get into the bidding. This is the kind of information you will absorb automatically with auctiongoing. But reading this chapter ahead of time may save you anxiety and even some money by helping you walk without stumbling right from the start.

An auction is physically comprised of a site, a staff, the clientele, and a selection of merchandise. Procedures, which vary only in detail from one auction to another, tie them all together into a sale. We have already discussed the great variety of indoor and outdoor locations for auctions. And by now you are quite familiar with the key person in all this, the auctioneer.

In this chapter is a description of the cast of characters and additional information that will help you prepare for and attend your first auction.

Finding the Right Auction

Once you know the kind of merchandise you are thinking of buying, locating a proper auction is a cinch. Even small cities have daily or weekly newspapers with want ads, where most auctions are announced. You may not find a heading reading "Auctions", but look under "Used Furniture", "Household Appliances", "Used Cars" or whatever fits your category. You may have to do this for several days before an auction notice appears. Keep in mind that these ads may be small, sometimes only a line or two setting forth the date, time and place of regularly scheduled auctions. For more information, follow up with a telephone call.

Sometimes you will find estate, jewelry, realty or government-sponsored auctions announced in larger display advertisements, usually in the newspaper section or pages devoted to news of business and finance.

Look also in the yellow pages of the telephone book under "Auctions" or "Auctioneers". If you find nothing suitable there, thumb through to other categories, such as "Furniture Dealers – Used".

These actions do not guarantee you'll discover what you're looking for. Some auction-houses don't advertise; they depend upon word-of-mouth among auction buffs and dealer/customers to spread the word of forthcoming events, which are almost always mentioned at any auction sale.

When traveling out of town, we have found that the managers of most used goods stores will willingly tell you where to locate local auctions, provided you ask tactfully. Most of these establishments get at least some of their goods at auction, although few customers would have reason to know that. But when you ask there about auctions, you mark yourself as knowledgeable. In our experience, few dealers show more than faint annoyance and will, even if with reluctance, respond to your question positively.

If you do find an auction that doesn't fit the category of goods you want, don't reject it out of hand. Few advertisements for auctions fully describe the range of merchandise. We once attended a "Jewelry Auction", for example, and took home two beautiful quilts. A telephone call to the auction-house will quickly clarify it all for you.

For readers interested in governmental auctions there are at least two printed sources in addition to *The Official Government Auction Guide,* by George Chelekis, cited earlier. Both are national in scope, so will be of little help to the novice with strictly local interests.

The first is *USA Auction Locator,* a periodical published monthly to set forth details of auctions held throughout the country. Most are government-sponsored, though some are private. The address: P.O. Box 674, Green Harbor, Mass. 02041. Subscription price: $48 per year.

Another periodic guide to auctions, mostly scheduled by governmental departments, is a newsletter published twice monthly and distributed by first-class mail to subscribers. It is *National Auction Bulletin, Inc.*, Fort Lauderdale, Fla. A year's subscription is $48.

The contents of both are comprised mainly of advertisements.

The Supporting Cast

Only in the rarest of situations is the auctioneer a one-man band. He needs people to serve customers as they arrive, to handle the merchandise, to keep track of the bidding, to assure order and honest dealing, to collect from the winning bidders, and to see that the goods sold are matched up with the proper buyers. Between auctions comes the matter of securing items from various sources for the next sale, with all that entails: soliciting, handling, tagging, storing, and arranging the merchandise; devising catalogs and distributing them, advertising when that's called for, and contacting potential customers by phone or mail.

The Clerk

From your point of view, the clerk is next in importance only to the auctioneer. She's an official (usually a woman, though occasionally a man) you need to watch. Her major duty is to record the winning bids on every item sold, whether in individual pieces or lots. This is busy work at a sizeable auction or a heavily-attended one. When the auctioneer uses a podium, the clerk usually is at his side, where she can view the entire house. If the auctioneer is a stroller, the clerk accompanies him, scribbling frequently on the papers fastened to her clipboard. That's how you will recognize her.

Her papers present information from the catalog, either as a list or a series of cards, identifying by name and number all the items to be offered at the auction. The clerk matches the winning bidder's number or name with the correct lot, along with the price. In some cases she also notes the runner-up bidder's identification too so that, if the winner defaults on the purchase, the auction-house knows who is next in line to be offered the merchandise. When you are ready to pick up your purchase and leave the auction, the clerk's record is verification to the cashier that you were the successful bidder. Her record-keeping is critical to the auction-house and you too have reason to want the work done well. The clerk is usually so busy that the auctioneer will commonly ask the audience not to talk to her during the auction. If no ringman is working, the clerk helps the auctioneer to spot bids.

The clerk's notations are forwarded ("sent up" in auction-house lingo) to the cashier for sorting out the data of who bought what. An errant clerk, or one distracted by customer questions, can make checking out of the auction a frustrating experience because of the confusion caused. This can also be the case when, at small auctions, the auctioneer attempts to handle the clerical task as well as his own.

We, and other regulars we know, keep lists of our own winning bids, recording at least the lot number and the dollar amount. If we make more than one purchase, we also write a short description of the item or lot for each. This is a double check on the clerk's work that we have found on occasion helps to speed up checking out.

The Ringman

At medium-to-large sales the auctioneer's efforts are bolstered by the work of a ringman (the term applies to both sexes), and at very large auctions there may be more than one of these. This individual shows, holds up, or otherwise displays merchandise, or at least describes it, before the auctioneer opens up the bidding. A principal activity for the ringman is to help the auctioneer spot bidders. This is particularly useful when the crowd is large and spread out or the action is rapid.

When a ringman spots a bid, a rousing "Yep!" may be heard, usually in informal sessions. At other times, the ringman may signal to the auctioneer that the asked price is offered by someone in the audience. Still other times, in very formal auction settings, the ringman may turn to the auctioneer and quietly observe, "I have $200". Being alert to the ringman may be as important as heeding the auctioneer. Watch the former and listen to the latter.

Some ringmen are apprentices who may spell the auctioneer at a break. When the ringman is not needed by the auctioneer as a spotter, he is likely to circulate around the room trying to arouse your enthusiasm to get into the bidding, talking up the merchandise, and generally stirring up the intensity of competition. His aim, of course, is to increase the house take. He's working strictly in the interest of the owner or manager. If you find him too pushy in this role, just ignore him. But when he is helping the auctioneer keep up with the bidding, he deserves your close attention.

Most ringmen are auction-house employees, who carry out other functions between sales. Others are part-timers with outside jobs. Here and there you'll find a ringman (male or female) who takes on the job just for the fun of it; that's mainly a labor of love for auction buffs. For example, a physician I know takes delight in working regularly as ringman in a formal auction-house, though he wears a beeper so as never to miss an emergency call to the hospital.

My husband and I have both served as ringmen for a particular jewelry-auction specialist who calls us in desperation. We are paid modestly for this but, alas, we usually spend more at the auction than we make. Which prompts me to explain for the benefit of novices that auction-house employees are generally permitted to participate in bidding on exactly the same basis as disinterested customers.

The word "ringman" is an interesting one but it is not defined in my dictionary. It probably derives from cattle auctions, which are held in a round arena or ring, with the critters being prodded in and out by a ringman.

The Cashier and Others

For all of us, the game stops at the cashier's desk. And for some, it's the first stop. At junk auctions and many other kinds, buying is a cash-and-carry proposition, although credit cards or checks are accepted at some. Don't show up expecting to pay that way, though, unless you've determined in advance that such a method of payment is accepted.

For big-ticket items at jewelry, art, estate, or antique auctions, the rules may require you to make a deposit with the cashier before you are registered to bid. Most houses make provision for you to be refunded upon departure by the cashier if you haven't tendered a winning bid. And mail-in auctions require that you submit a cashier's check or the equivalent for a portion of your bid, often ten percent. At any rate, if you have any questions about the financial end of the auction transaction, the cashier is the person to pose them to. So he or she may be the first employee of the house with whom you deal, as well as the last.

When you check out, the cashier collects all the bid cards designating your purchases that were filled in by the clerk.Totaling them, the cashier arrives at your purchase price. After you've paid, the cashier hands you copies of the bid notes. You want to examine them for accuracy (honest mistakes are not uncommon and dishonesty is always possible) because you must present them as proof of purchase when you pick up the merchandise. If you are a dealer or re-seller, they become your records of purchase for accounting and tax purposes.

In small auction businesses each employee may play multiple roles. The checker is responsible for seeing to it that you get the merchandise you have purchased by pairing your bid notes with whatever you are toting off, or that you may ask the house to hold for later pickup. This same checker may also be a warehouseman (rarely a woman) who spends much time receiving, storing, tagging, and arranging the goods to be sold, and it's also possible that he will serve as a clerk or ringman during the auction. If you have arranged for your purchase to be delivered, you may find the same person pulling a truck into your driveway, hauling the goods.

The utilization of staff in any auction-house is a function of size and volume of activity. The examples here are typical but not all-inclusive, but I hope they are instructive.

Delivery of Purchases

Home or store delivery is not always available but when it isn't, the auction house usually can make arrangements for you. There aren't too many families readily equipped to manhandle a refrigerator or, for that matter, a ton of bricks, although the sale of such items is commonplace. And if you buy a grandfather clock or another goody that demands expert handling, you may hesitate to risk using your own station wagon or pickup truck.

Auction-houses with frequent sales or consistent high volume find it worthwhile to maintain their own delivery capability. When this is the case, you can expect prompt and efficient service – but you may have to pay a fee for it. If your aim is to bid in a piano, a dining room set or something else awkward to handle, you'd be well-advised to find out in advance how it will be delivered and what the cost will be. That'll save you the embarrassment of making a great buy on the auction floor and then losing your shirt to get it into the home.

Registration

As you enter most auction places, you will be asked to give your name, address, telephone number, and other pertinent information. That accomplished, you will at most houses be handed an identification card – usually containing a number – that you raise during the auction when you enter a bid. It simplifies work for the clerk to note down a number rather than ask for your name. But you have to remember to keep it out of sight during the bidding process, lest displaying it be interpreted as making a bid. At the same time, you usually also receive a catalog and an information sheet detailing the rules of the auction-house.

The other information that may be solicited can relate to your credit and to your business status. If this discloses that you own a store or are otherwise a dealer, your purchase may not be subject to sales tax; the assumption is that the ultimate retail buyer will pay the tax. This varies from state to state according to law but can be an element in your cost.

While this is the common experience, it must be said that not all auctions require registration. Fred and I attend some at which attendees call out their bids. The winner's name is recorded by the clerk by name rather than bid card number. And in most such cases, there is no catalog; either you make note in advance of the lot numbers you are interested in, or you bid without further identification on whatever item or lot the auctioneer, clerk or ringman has indicated as the subject of the current sale.

Whatever the system, you should experience little trouble with it. If you expect to spend more than the amount of cash you care to carry with you, save yourself time and nervous energy by checking in advance with the cashier to assure that whatever means you intend to use to pay for your purchases is acceptable.

Food Service

Attending an auction can be like going to a play. It often comes off late in the afternoon or in the evening, and you must decide when to squeeze in your regular meal. Should you grab a bite in advance – or wait until afterwards?

Well, sometimes you can down snacks or a meal right on the auction-house premises. One auction we regularly attend provides a catered supper so good that we look forward to it as part of the period set aside for inspection of the merchandise. Don't count on this degree of service. The availability, kind and quality of food service varies from nil to excellent.

At some auctions, you'll find a mobile sandwich truck stationed outside. Some houses offer snack foods for the taking, while others will serve complimentary wine or other drinks, and still others simply provide coin machine food or drink dispensers. Most auctions want to provide just enough to assure you won't stay away for lack of sustenance, but have no aspirations to achieve reputations for good cuisine.

If you have a conflict between hunger pangs and the urge to find a steal, check in advance with the auction-house. You may discover the virtue of bringing along your own brown-bag special.

Pocketbook Issues

Think of auction-houses as you would of specialty stores. You don't go to Sotheby's or Christie's to buy used clothing. Nor would you go to a junk auction to find a ruby necklace. You consider your needs and match them to your bank book when considering buying at auction. Our lawyer friend who collects oriental rugs spends more at a specialty auction for a single purchase than we do at dozens of auctions over the course of a year. And there is little point in attending a real estate auction if you are in the market for a used car. So there is more than price involved in selecting the proper auction for your needs. But once you have decided to attend an auction with intent to buy, you do need to consider how you're going to manage the cost.

We know people at or barely above the poverty line who buy at auction, and we admire them for being astute enough to do so. It stretches limited budgets. We don't often attend auctions appealing to the wealthy because the prices are outside our means, although curiosity alone sometimes draws us in as spectators. The vast majority of auctiongoers we run up against are neither rich nor poor; they have limited budgets, including business persons, collectors, amateurs and auction buffs like ourselves.

We have attended many auctions with a budget of under $25, and have left with change, carrying out amazing arrays of purchases. We budget for auctions much as some do for entertainment. We'll pass up dinner at an expensive restaurant and commit the funds to auction-buying. With experience, we've learned to accumulate funds for the purpose by selling some of the things we acquire, always at a reasonable profit. This has led us to pick up some items at auction with deliberate intent to resell them, while at the same time we also purchase things we want to use privately. And I must admit we sell even some of those private-use items if the right price is offered.

Nearly everybody who regularly shops at auction has, or develops, a philosophy for doing so. At the outset, ours was quite simple. We wanted to acquire both practical and luxury items that we could otherwise not afford or that represented a substantial saving over retail without an equivalent sacrifice of quality. Quality, of course, is a subjective matter. Some of the antiques we have bought, for example, required restorative work on our part, but otherwise would have been nearly impossible to come by except at auction – and we snagged them for peanuts.

As our experience accumulated, we began also to buy merchandise at bargain prices that we knew we could resell at a profit to help subsidize purchases for ourselves and family. As this activity grew modestly, word got around the neighborhood and we began to get requests to look for particular items. When we found them, below the price these friends and acquaintances were willing to pay, we purchased them and added a surcharge. This did three things for us: (1) it helped cement friendships; (2) it added to our auction kitty, and (3) it established for us a modest part-time business that can be carried out more as a hobby than an enterprise, combining the best of two worlds, since participating in auctions is – to us – fun.

To many, auction-going is simply another means of shopping, and some consider it more of a chore than a pleasure. When that's the case, the auction advantage is sheerly economic. But it is easy for one to get hooked on the suspense and excitement of the process, as well as the satisfaction of beating the financial odds. At most auctions you pay by cash, check or credit card, avoiding the high interest of installment payments for big-ticket items on the kind of plans offered by retailers.

You will not know just how the auction experience will impact on your financial life until you have tried it. The only certainty is that, if you don't let the fever run away with you, you can expect the immediate benefit of saving money, while perhaps enjoying some purchase that might otherwise have been impractical. But the growing popularity of auctions is at least partially due to additional opportunities they open up for men and women to earn pin money, or to increase their savings for other purposes, or even to go into business. It's a thought that rarely enters the heads of first-time attendees but sometimes accretes with exposure.

Whatever your aim, we can appreciate the impulse from which it stems. And we wish you all the luck in the world.

APPENDIX

Contents

Brief Glossary of Auction Terms

absolute auction. All merchandise put up to bid will be sold regardless of winning prices.

add-ons. Other lots to be sold will be placed to bid with the offered lot. "Let's <u>add on</u> to this lot."

as is, where is. There is no guarantee of the quality or workability of the merchandise. "All merchandise will be sold <u>as is, where is</u> at this auction."

back-up (bidder). A non-winning bid. "Is my <u>back-up bidder</u> interested in purchasing any of the other pieces in this lot?"

bid card. A card with identification number or name assigned to attendee. "Use your <u>bid card</u> to signal the auctioneer when you want to make an offer on a lot."

brother-in-law bids. Identifies offers in which apparent competitors are not really competing. Often used between friends or family members to make sure one wins the bid. This is unethical. "That looks like a <u>brother-in-law bid</u> to me."

buyer's choice. When more than one similar item is part of a lot, the winning bidder will have first choice in the number of items or best quality among the items. "<u>Buyer's choice</u> on these necklaces allows the winning bidder to take one or all of the merchandise."

buyer's premium. A charge added to the winning price offered. "There will be a five percent <u>buyer's premium</u> added to the accepted bid price."

call it as we see it. The auctioneer's or house's claim that the business will identify quality of merchandise as it is brought to the floor; usually associated with defects in merchandise. "We call it as we see it."

closed bids. Bids given the auction-house on specific lots by absentees. The house makes the bids on their behalf. "We'll be making closed bids of some individuals."

contents only. The statement that the container or display table is not included in the bidding for the merchandise. "The jewelry lot is sold contents only."

consign. To place merchandise for sale at auction by a second party who agrees to pay a fee upon sale. "I will consign my porcelain collection to an auction house."

each. Similar items in a single lot will be sold at the winning bid price, indicating bids taken on a per-item basis. "Every item in this lot will be paid for as if each item is purchased separately." (See "times the money".)

finger/ hand signal bids. A system of hand signals specifing bid amounts or lot numbers. Rarely used except by professional auction attendees. "The finger/hand signals indicate $150."

hold bid. Applies to individual items in a lot comprised of a number of pieces, such as a set of furniture. High bids hold each item provisionally. The auctioneer may then offer the entire set as a unit and will award it to the high bidder if that bid exceeds the total of the individually priced pieces. "This bedroom set will be sold on a hold bid."

house. Another term for an auction business. "The house reserves the right to accept or reject all bids."

letter of credit. An official document issued by a bank or other savings institution to a bidder that assures the seller of the buyer's credit-worthiness.

looks like. A term used to identify merchandise that bears close resemblance to work done, most often, by well-known manufacturers, designers, etc. Often associated with antiques. It's the house's disclaimer of responsibility for the origin of the merchandise. "This porcelain looks like a genuine Enoch Wood piece."

lot/lots. Identifies an item or a group of items tagged and offered as a single object for bid. "This lot number is 129 and contains books, dishes, and other miscellaneous items." Or, "We know you are interested in lot number 130, the hand-made quilt."

minimum (bid). Identifies a lot on which the house sets the lowest price it will entertain as the opening bid. "We have a $200 minimum on this bracelet."

nod. A signal sometimes used by a bidder to indicate his acceptance of a called price. Commonly used in the absence of bid cards. "We'll try and recognize nods in the bidding but, if we don't, call out your bid."

open high. The practice by some auctioneers to ask for opening bids at a rate higher than it is likely will be offered by attendees. "The auctioneer regularly opens high."

open low. Opposite of open high.

reconsign. A buyer may elect to return the merchandise to the auction-house for sale at a later auction, for a fee. "We do accept <u>reconsigned</u> goods."

registration. Attendees' checking-in process, when the name and address are recorded, bid card and catalog issued and other preliminaries (if any) are taken care of.

reserve. Merchandise that has been assigned a lowest price that will be accepted in bids. "We have a <u>reserve</u> on this lot."

ringman. Identifies an individual who assists the auctioneer in identifying bidders and in other ways. "Our <u>ringman</u> for this evening is Sam Jones."

sealed bids. See "closed bids".

takes one, takes all. A phrase that informs attendees that regardless of the bid, the winning bidder is required to take all of the merchandise. Often "times the money". "This lot of sixteen typewriters is offered <u>takes one; takes all</u>."

times the money: An offer to purchase a single lot may require payment for each of the items at the same price as the single item purchased. "Sold! $27.50, <u>times the money</u> on six chairs."

upon approval. The consignor has stipulated the lowest acceptable price. A dishonest auction-house may claim an item is to be sold upon approval when it is actually the property of the auction-house. A dodge to avoid selling at a loss. "We can sell this item only <u>upon approval</u> of its owner."

State Governing Agencies

Alabama*
Alabama State Board of
Examiners
P.O.Box 1207
Cullman, AL 35056

Alaska
Division of Occupational
Licensing
3601 C Street, Suite 722
Anchorage AL 99503

Arizona
Department of Revenue
License & Registration
Section
1600 W. Monroe
Phoenix AR 85007

Arkansas*
Auctioneers Licensing Board
221 W. Second, Suite 230
Little Rock AR 72201

California*
Auctioneer Commission
2231 J St., Suite 101
Sacramento CA 98516

Colorado
Division of Real Estate
1776 Logan Street
Denver CO 80203

Connecticut
Dept. of Consumer Protec-
tion/Real Estate
165 Capitol Ave., Rm G8
Hartford CT 06106

Delaware*
Division of Revenue
Carvel State Office Bldg.
820 N. French St.
Wilmington DE 19801

District of Columbia*
Dept. of Consumer &
Regulatory Affairs
614 H. St., N.W.
Washington DC 20001

Florida*
Dept. of Professional Regn.
1940 N. Monroe St.
Tallahassee FL 32399

Georgia*
Auctioneers Commission
166 Pryor St., S.W.
Atlanta GA 30303

Hawaii*
City & County of Honolulu
Dept of Finance, MV&L
1455 S. Beretania St.
Honolulu HI 96814

Idaho*
Refer questions to local
county treasurer

Illinois
Office of the Governor
Springfield IL 62706

Indiana*
Professional Licensing
Agency
1021 Indiana Govt. Center
North
100 N. Senate Ave.
Indianapolis IN 46204

Iowa
Dept. of Agriculture & Land
Stewardship
Wallace Building
Des Moines IA 50319

Kansas*
Ofc. of Attorney General
Kansas Judicial Center
Topeka KS 66612

Kentucky*
Board of Auctioneers
400 Sherburn Lane
Louisville KY 40207

Louisiana*
Auctioneers Licensing Board
8017 Jefferson Highway,
Suite B-3
Baton Rouge LA 70809

Maine*
Dept. of Professional &
Financial Regulation
State House Station #35
Augusta ME 04333

Maryland*
Refer questions to local
county governments

Massachusetts*
Division of Standards
One Ashburton Place
Boston MA 02108

Michigan
Bur. of Occupation & Profes-
sional Regulation
Real Estate Board
P.O. Box 30018
Lansing MI 48909

Minnesota*
Refer questions to local
county governments

Mississippi
Secretary of State
P.O. Box 136
Jackson MS 39205

Missouri*
Refer questions to local
county clerks.

Montana
Department of Commerce
1424 Ninth Avenue
Helena MT 59620

Nebraska
Real Estate Commission
P.O. 94667
Lincoln NE 68509

Nevada
Real Estate Division
1665 Hot Springs Road
Las Vegas NV 89710

New Hampshire*
Board of Auctioneers
Secretary of State office
State House, Room 204
Concord NH 03301

New Jersey
Refer questions to local city
or county government.

New Mexico*
Regulation & Licensing
Department
725 St. Michael's Drive
Santa Fe NM 87504

New York
Office of Business Permits
AESOB, 17th Flr.
P.O. Box 7027
Albany NY 12225

North Carolina*
Auctioneer Licensing Board
Suite 306, Haworth Bldg.
3509 Haworth Drive
Raleigh NC 27609

North Dakota*
Public Service Commission
Grain Elevator Division
State Capitol
Bismarck ND 58505

Ohio*
Dept. of Commerce, Division
of Licensing
77 S. High Street, 23rd floor
Columbus OH 43266

Oklahoma*
Refer questions to local
county treasurers.

Oregon
Real Estate Agency
158 12th St., N.E., 2nd Floor
Salem OR 97310

Pennsylvania*
Bd. of Auctioneer Examiners
P.O. Box 2649
Harrisburg PA 17105

Rhode Island*
Dept. of Business Regulation
233 Richmond St., Suite 230
Providence RI 02903

South Carolina*
Auctioneer's Commission
1200 Main Street, Suite 301
Columbia SC 29201

South Dakota*
Real Estate Commission
P.O. Box 490
Pierre SD 57501

Tennessee*
Dept. of Commerce and
Insurance
500 James Robertson Pkwy.
Nashville TN 37243

Texas*
Dept. of Licensing and
Regulation
P.O. Box 12157
Austin TX 78711

Utah
Department of Commerce
P.O. Box 45802
Salt Lake City UT 84145

Vermont*
Office of Professional
Regulation
109 State Street
Montpelier VT 05609

Virginia*
Department of Commerce
3600 W. Broad Street
Richmond VA 23230

Washington*
Professional Licensing
Services
P.O. Box 9020
Olympia WA 98507

West Virginia*
Department of Agriculture,
Marketing & Development
East Wing, State Capitol
Charleston WV 25305

Wisconsin
Department of Regulation
and Licensing
P.O. Box 8935
Madison WI 53708

Wyoming
Attorney General
123 Capitol Building
Cheyenne WY 82002

* States requiring licenses.
Qualifications vary some-
what from state to state.

Cost of First House Furnished
(See Chapter One)

Item	Price paid	Used	New
Living room			
Tweed sofa	$30	$75	$300
Coffee table	12	25	50
End table	7	25	50
Rocker	25	40	70
Antique sewing			
machine	45	90	300
Easy chair	15	30	150
Pair lamps	15	30	60
Den			
Tweed sofa	30	75	300
Coffee table	12	25	50
Chair	18	35	80
TV (portable)	90	150	300
End table	8	25	80
TV stand	5	15	30
Chair	12	25	60
Lamp	8	20	30
Dining room			
Table/6 chairs, buffet	75	200	700
Kitchen			
Table/4 chairs	60	140	200
Refrigerator	100	150	500
Dishes/glasses	30	80	150
Pots/pans	20	30	200
Flatware/utensils	15	25	125
Bdrm (master)			
Bed/mattress/springs	50	100	400
Dresser	30	75	150
Lamp	12	20	30
Highboy	60	90	200

Cost of First House (Cont'd)

Item	Price Paid	Used	New
Bdrm (small)			
Twin bed	30	80	150
Dresser	25	50	150
Lamp	5	10	30
Bdrm #3			
Bed (full)	40	100	200
Dresser	35	60	150
Lamp	7	20	30
Fabrics			
Assorted	30	60	150
Pillows	15	50	100
Paint	20	40	150
Totals	**$988**	**$2066**	**$5645**

Note: Used and new figures represent approximate selling prices current at the time we made these purchases.

Cost of Furnishing Second House

In this chart we present similar information on the cost of furnishing the coast house, also indicating the kind of auction at which we bid in these items.

Type Auction	Item	Price Paid	Price New
General	Queen bed	$75	$200
General	Easy chair	25	200
General	Bedside table	15	75
Junk	Lamp	8	25
Estate	Bedspread (blue quilt)	12	40
Antique	Trundle bed	50	200
Junk	2 fold-out chair/beds	20	60
Junk	Hanging lamp	8	30
Antique	Buffet (linen storage)	40	300
Estate	Bookcase	25	150
Junk	Sofa hide-a-bed	30	300
Junk	Sofa	50	400
Estate	Faux oriental rug	55	400
Junk	Table/4 chairs	40	200
Antique	4-poster bed	100	500
Estate	Table/4 chairs	75	500
Estate	Sleeper/sofa (single)	40	200
Junk	TV (19" portable color)	80	400
Junk	2 Recliner chairs	85	500
Specialty	Fishing equipment	120	400
	Totals	**$953**	**$5080**

Our Own Home Furnishings:
Items bought at Auction

Throughout this book, I have referred to furniture and decorative items we have acquired at auctions for bargain prices. I make no attempt here to itemize them all. This is a list of purchases that might be sought by any consumer, set forth in the hope it will give readers a reasonably accurate idea of what they might expect to find, about what it might cost them, and the equivalent prices for similar items if purchased new at retail.

A note of caution: We have spent some years in the process of accumulation, so there is no assurance that prices may not have changed. The estimated values given here are arrived at, in part, through actual assessment of antiques by experts, and in part simply by comparing our purchase prices with those prevailing at the time in retail outlets or antique stores.

<u>Our Home Furnishings</u>

Gobelin tapestry 3 1/2x4	27	1,000
Grandfather clock	295	850
6 pc. Eastlake parlor set	350	3,500
Upholstery for above	100	
Brass trunk	40	90
Painted rosewood coffee table	75	300
Bronze crystal candleholders		
with carved wooden candles	12	150
Oriental tea table/4 stools	70	500
Pitcher/basin (Johnson Bros.)	25	200
Floor lamp, touch	2	75
Curio cabinet	125	500
Chest, ivory+inlay	70	400
Antique crazy quilt	10	850
Shirley Temple dolls (2 signed)	50	500
Area rug	45	400
Singer sewing machine (antique)	45	175
Silk cherry blossom trees (4)	68	375

Stained glass windows (4)	100	400
Chair, hand-carved mahogany	10	90
English buffet	80	300
Dn. room table/6 chairs/Drexel	295	3,500
Re-cover chairs	90	
Bronze/crystal chandelier	125	325
China cabinet	90	700
Tables, 3 nested/scrimshaw	125	400
Tea cart, scrimshaw	50	300
9x12 Oriental rug/rose	150	800
Hutch/Drexel copy	225	1,500
Table (top only)	23	90
Leather rolling chairs (4)	80	800
Window seat/Welsh	60	400
Maple desk, single pedestal	15	75
Metal table lamp	2	25
Avon bottles (pre-1960s)	27	400
Microwave hutch	45	200
Rocker, hardrock maple	50	300
Bar stools, white leather (2)	34	150
Lv. room set, 3 pc. (new)	125	600
Boudoir lamps, teal cut glass	15	130
Blanket box	35	200
Television 21", color	80	150
Night stands, wood, tall (2)	30	50
Rag rugs, imported, 2 runners	20	100
Organ, Thomas, solid state	900	400
Love seat, leather, antique	90	500
Sofa sectional, leatherette	5	200
Bookcases, (3)	150	500
Area rug, mideast import	35	200
Coffee table, swing/bar	65	300
3' Brass candlestands (2)	10	100
Armoire, child's	40	125
Platform rocker	11	50
Bdrm set, new, w/highboy, chest		
mattress, springs	325	800
Area rug, oriental style	30	200
Bookcases (2)	10	200
Desks (2)	10	100

Computer, software, screen, printer, IBM clone/new	600	3,000
Area rug 12x15	50	200
Bookcase	5	20
Armoire, child's	40	125
Sewing machine/cabinet/French provincial/new	600	800
Menu board	5	100
Entertainment center	80	300
Chamber chairs (3) antique	125	400
Wallpaper (for entire house)	50	500
Totals	**$9,886**	**$30,970**

Regional Federal Information Offices

These offices, provided by the General Services Administration, can tell the caller where to find the federal government sales outlets nearest your home or business. The toll-free 800 numbers provided are applicable only within the cities and states listed. If you are calling from another location, the number is 301/ 722-9098. An alternative is to mail your inquiry to Federal Information Center, P.O. Box 600, Cumberland MD 21502.

Alabama
Birmingham, Mobile
800/366-2998

Alaska
Anchorage
800/729-8003

Arkansas
Little Rock
800/366-2998

California
Los Angeles, San Diego,
San Francisco, Santa Ana
800/726-4995
Sacramento
800/973-1695

Colorado
Colorado Springs,
Denver, Pueblo
800/399-3997

Connecticut
Hartford, New Haven
800/3471997

Florida
Ft. Lauderdale, Jacksonville, Miami, Orlando, St. Petersburg, Tampa,
West Palm Beach
800/347-1997

Georgia
Atlanta
800/347-1997

Hawaii
Honolulu
800/733-5996

Illinois
Chicago
800/366-2998

Indiana
Gary
800/366-2998
Indianapolis
800/347-1997

Iowa
All locations
800/735-8004

Kansas
All locations
800/735-8004

Kentucky
Louisville
800/347-1997

Lousiana
New Orleans
800/366-2998

Maryland
Baltimore
800/ 347-1997

Massachusetts
Boston
800/347-1997

Michigan
Detroit, Grand Rapids
800/347-1997

Minnesota
Minneapolis
800/366-2998

Missouri
St. Louis
800/366-2998
All other locations
800/735-8004

Nebraska
Omaha
800/366-2998
All other locations
800/735-8004

New Jersey
Newark, Trenton
800/347-1997

New Mexico
Albuquerque
800/359-3997

New York
Albany, Buffalo, New
York, Rochester, Syra-
cuse
800/347-1997

North Carolina
Charlotte
800/347-1997

Ohio
Akron, Cincinnati,
Cleveland, Columbus,
Dayton, Toledo
800/347-1997

Pennsylvania
Philadelphia, Pittsburgh
800/347-1997

165

Rhode Island
Providence
800/347-1997

Tennessee
Chattanooga
800/347-1997
Memphis, Nashville
800/366-2998

Texas
Austin, Dallas, Fort
Worth, Houston, San
Antonio
800/366-2998

Utah
Salt Lake City
800/347-1997

Virginia
Norfolk, Richmond,
Roanoke
800/347-1997

Washington
Seattle, Tacoma
800/726-4995

Wisconsin
800/366-2998